D. Scott Rogo serves on the graduate faculty of John F. Kennedy University in Orinda, California. He has worked as a visiting researcher at the (former) Division of Parapsychology and Psychophysics of Maimonides Medical Center in Brooklyn, New York, and the Psychical Research Foundation in Durham, North Carolina. He has written some 20 books on the paranormal, and he is a consulting editor for *Fate* magazine.

Books by D. Scott Rogo

LEAVING THE BODY: A Complete Guide to Astral Projection (1983)
OUR PSYCHIC POTENTIALS (1984)
ON THE TRACK OF THE POLTERGEIST (1985)
THE SEARCH FOR YESTERDAY: A Critical Examination of the
  Evidence for Reincarnation (1985)

LEAVING
THE
BODY

*A Complete Guide
to Astral Projection*

D. Scott Rogo

A FIRESIDE BOOK
Published by Simon & Schuster
New York London Toronto Sydney Tokyo Singapore

FIRESIDE
Simon & Schuster Building
Rockefeller Center
1230 Avenue of the Americas
New York, New York 10020

Copyright © 1983 by Prentice Hall Press

Published in 1986 by Prentice Hall Press
Originally published by Prentice-Hall, Inc.
First Fireside Edition 1993
FIRESIDE and colophon are trademarks of
Simon & Schuster Inc.

Manufactured in the United States of America

23 25 27 29 30 28 26 24 22

Library of Congress Cataloging in Publication Data
Rogo, D. Scott.
Leaving the body.

Includes bibliographies and index.
I. Astral projection.   I. Title.
BF1389.A7R63 1983 133.9 82-13273
ISBN 0-671-76394-6

To Richard Parks—who wanted to learn

and

To Dr. John Palmer—who wanted to understand

Contents

Clung: cling: hold on tightly to.
remnant: (remnant / remaining.

Foreword

Do you have a soul?

Will any part of you survive death?

If you believe you have some kind of soul, that some part of you will survive death, how do you know your belief isn't superstitious nonsense, fearfully clung to by you because you can't face up to the inevitability and finality of death?

Questions about having a soul that would survive death were once vital to people in our society. Most people, educated and uneducated alike, believed some part of themselves would survive death. Today the word *soul* is seldom mentioned in educated circles, and the whole idea of soul is treated like a remnant from more primitive times, a psychological compensation that might have been needed when life was more uncertain, brutal, and ignorant, but which is certainly unnecessary to enlightened people of our day.

It is true that the idea of a soul can be used as a way of avoiding the realities of life, but then any idea can be used in that way. If we really do have some sort of soul that may survive death, the consequences are enormous for how we view ourselves and others and for how we want to live our lives. Aside from the strange psychological uses people have put the idea of soul to, what are the facts about the idea of soul?

You can study the history of the *concept* of soul, what people have thought about it, the derivation of the word soul, and you can reason about how the concept of soul does or does not make "sense." As Roger Bacon, one of the founders of science, said, though, "There are two modes of knowing: through argument and experience. Argument brings conclusions and compels us to concede them, but does not cause certainty nor remove doubts in order that the mind may remain at rest in truth, unless this is provided by experience." Fundamentally, the basis of the concept of soul is not an *idea*, but an *experience*. Thousands, if not millions, of people alive today have had the experience of existing outside the space of their physical bodies for a brief period and experiencing this separated state as *real*, not as a dream or imaginary experience. A typical consequence of such an out-of-the-body experience is on the order of "I no longer *believe* that I have a soul, or that some part of me will survive death, I know it!" Ideas about souls exist because people have had overwhelming, often life-altering experiences of existing beyond the limits of their physical bodies.

Scholarly and scientific studies of other people's experiences are valuable. One of the most satisfying accomplishments of my career has been that my experimental studies of a talented out-of-body experiencer, "Miss Z," helped to initiate a new era of scientific studies of out-of-the-body experiences (see *Journal of the American Society for Psychical Research*, 1968, pp. 3-27). She was able to produce an OBE for me in my laboratory as I monitored her brain waves and other physiological functions. But for many people, studies of others' experiences can never carry enough conviction about an idea so opposed by current cultural fashions as out-of-the-body experiences. We want direct, personal experience. That is where this book will be very helpful.

D. Scott Rogo has done us all a great service by collecting sets of techniques which may induce out-of-the-body experiences in many people. By extensive search through a literature that is unknown to most people, Rogo has collected, analyzed, and distilled the essences of a variety of psychological techniques that may lead to out-of-the-body experiences. There is no other book like this one in covering such potentially valuable material, and in being so sensible in covering material that is easily sensationalized.

Suppose you diligently practice one or more of the techniques in this book? Suppose it works? One night you find yourself free of your physical body, obviously alive and conscious, no longer limited by the boundaries of physical existence: what then? A great adventure awaits!

Charles T. Tart Ph.D.
Department of Psychology
University of California, Davis

Preface

Astral projection, the ability to "leave the body" at will, is a phenomenon that has long fascinated the general public. Not only are books on the subject popular best-sellers, but many people have long clamored for information about how the experience can be induced and learned. As some one who has been a student of the subject for many years, I am still constantly amazed at the number of requests I get for this type of information.

If the general public has long searched for this information, a number of organizations have amassed fortunes by profiteering from this interest. The most visible of these is the *Eckankar* organization, founded in California in the 1960s by the late Paul Twitchell. Twitchell (who relied heavily on ghost-writers) wrote several tracts on his out-of-body adventures and the Eckankar movement built up around him. The movement promises that, for a fee, the initiate will be trained in the cult's cosmology and astral projection techniques. Unfortunately, the Eckankar people have never published any hard core data demonstrating that their techniques work. These techniques—which range from meditation, to mantra yoga, to imagery exercises—are, however, part and parcel of traditional astral projection lore and probably do work for at least some people. Over the years I have received many letters from disciples of the movement who claim they have learned to induce out-of-body experiences through these teachings. Since these methods are pretty basic and are not unique to the Eckankar movement, however, it hardly seems worthwhile for anyone to dish out large sums of money in order to procure them. Nor is it necessary to prescribe to the Eckankar's hodgepodge cosmology of popular occultism, Eastern philosophy, and metaphysics to enjoy the experience.

Another organization that has been quick to capitalize on the public interest in astral projection is the *American Research Team* in Beverly Hills, California. Despite its impressive title, the Team is actually nothing more than an agency that sells a tape of electronic sounds that they claim induces out-of-body experiences. The group maintains that they have evidence that their tape works, but have yet to make any such documentation public. When I first heard the tape, in fact, I was serving on the editorial staff of *Psychic* magazine and quipped to my editors that the tape made you want to leave the body to escape from it! The editors had turned the tape over to me because they wanted my advice on whether or not we should run an ad for it. My advice was that the ad was misleading. The promoters claimed that *anyone* could have an out-of-body experience by merely listening to the tape, but they could offer no substantiation in this regard.

Techniques on leaving the body have also been taught by several so-called "mind-dynamics" organization such as Silva Mind Control and the various spin-offs spawned by this very popular program.

These attempts to commercialize the existence of procedures for inducing out-of-body travel were a guiding force in my desire to produce a complete yet inexpensive guide to the *genuine* procedures.

My second reason for writing this book comes from my personal interest in the out-of-body experience. I began studying parapsychology seriously while still a teenager. When I first read about astral projection, I decided that this was something I wanted to learn how to do! I waded through scores of books on the subject, hoping to find some magic formula that would make the practice easy and reliable. Well...it wasn't that easy. What resulted was over two years of experimentation with various systems, and I was more than gratified when I had my first out-of-body experience one summer day in 1965.

This initial incident was the first of many I had over the next two years, and sporadically until this day. It was during these two years that I learned to partially control and even induce these strange journeys of the mind. So to some extent, I was indeed able to learn how to induce out-of-body travel. Since I have never considered myself particularly psychic, there is no reason not to believe that anyone can learn to induce the experience on his or her own.

My interest in learning to leave the body was renewed in 1973 when I was offered a visiting research consultantship with the Psychical Research Foundation in Durham, North Carolina. The P.R.F. had received a grant to study the out-of-body experience and was working with S. Keith Harary, a gifted Duke student, who could induce these experiences at will. Since Mr. Harary could leave the body while remaining awake, I became most interested in the procedures he was using to make his dramatic exits. I had many discussions with him on the subject. Later in my career I met Ingo Swann, a New York psychic who also can induce mind travel at will. Once again I found myself asking him many questions about just how he did it.

Gradually I began codifying all this information. How do these techniques compare and contrast? Does one particular procedure work better than any other? Is astral projection like a skill that one learns to control through practice, trial and error? These were many of the issues I began thinking about.

This book is therefore devoted to several different systems which allegedly help one leave the body. I am not saying that all of them work. But some evidence *does* exist showing that each of these techniques will probably work for some people.

Because of the controversial nature of these techniques, each of the main chapters of this book will be divided into three major sections. In the first section I will explain how each procedure was devised and the rationale behind it. After explaining the actual technique in as much detail as possible, I will critically evaluate each system and cite any pertinent evidence I know of that the system either works or does not. As I mentioned earlier, most of these techniques probably will work for a limited number of individuals. Some people may find one particular method works, while others may have success with several of them. Yet even others may find that none of them work.

It should be continually emphasized, in this regard, that the key word to this volume is *responsibility*. No outrageous promises can be made, nor do I make them. (Nor could I sanction any particular method of out-of-body induction.) This book is intended primarily as a layman's guide to the out-of-body experience, geared toward that segment of the public that sincerely wants to learn the valid techniques of astral projection.

D. Scott Rogo
Northridge, California

ACKNOWLEDGMENTS

Extracts from Celia Green's *Out-of-the Body Experiences* © 1968 by the Institute for Psychophysical Research is reprinted by permission of the I.P.R., Oxford, England, distributed in the U.S.A. and Canada by State Mutual Book & Periodical Service Ltd., 521 Fifth Ave., New York, N.Y 10017, U.S.A.

Extracts from Raynor Johnson's *A Watcher on the Hills* © 1959 by Raynor C. Johnson is reprinted by permission of Hodder and Stoughton Limited, London.

Material from Sylvan Muldoon and Hereward Carrington's *The Projection of the Astral Body* is reprinted with permission of Samuel Weiser, Inc., New Beach, Maine.

Quotations from Richard A. Greene's *The Handbook of Astral Projection*— © 1979 by Richard A. Greene—are reprinted by permission of Next Step Publications, P.O. Box 1403, Nashua, New Hampshire 03061.

Portions of Chapter One originally appeared as the article "Psychiatry Investigates OBEs" in the April 1982 issue of *Fate* and are adopted here by special permission of the editors.

chapter one
The
Out-of-Body
Potential

It's been a long day, and you're tired. You come home, nearly doze off in front of the television set, then wander down the hall and plop on your bed expecting to fall asleep in an instant. But—suddenly and mysteriously—you find yourself paralyzed. Gushing sounds fill your ears. Bright flashes of light flicker under your closed eyelids. Then you feel as if you are beginning to float.

A moment later, you open your eyes and find yourself hovering above your body. You *are* floating in the air! You are able to examine your physical body and everything else in the room from this viewpoint and independent perspective. Your mind seems totally released from the confines of the body and you feel a freedom and expanded sense of awareness you have never experienced before. But just as you are beginning to orient yourself to this new and novel state of being, you have a momentary "blackout." Within a fraction of a second, you "awake" back inside your body.

If this has ever happened to you, you are not alone. The experience may have been frightening, transcendent, or merely puzzling. But it was not unique. Millions of people have undergone this strange adventure, which has been variously called astral projection, out-of-body travel, ESP projection, and a host of other things.

It is unfortunately true, however, that the classic out-of-body experience (or OBE for short) does vaguely resemble certain phenomena studied in psychiatry and abnormal psychology. A psychiatrist reading the above account might classify it as an example of depersonalization (a feeling that the self is no longer real), distortion of body image (where the sense of the body's boundaries becomes confused), or autoscopy (the seeing of one's own apparition). The OBE is markedly different from these anomalies of perception in one great—and vastly important—way, however. It is often *veridical*, or truth-telling. In other words, if you were to "leave the body" and travel to a location miles away, you might be able to correctly see what was going on there! This aspect of the OBE takes it out of the hands of the psychiatrist and into those of the parapsychologist and those scientists who study the strange byways of psychic phenomena.

Take the following instance, for example, which was sent to Celia Green of the Institute of Psychophysical Research in Oxford, England. The sender was a woman who had just had an operation for peritonitis. Complications had set in and pneumonia had developed. Since she was in an L-shaped ward, she could see nothing beyond the bend in the hallway. Yet . . .

"One morning," the woman writes, "I felt myself floating upward and found I was looking down on the rest of the patients. I could see myself; propped up against pillows, very white and ill. I saw the sister and nurse rush to my bed with oxygen." While out-of-body, she saw a woman down the hall sitting up in bed. This was a location beyond the capability of her physical view. The patient had bandages wrapped around her head and was knitting something with blue wool. She had a very red face. The astonished out-of-body traveler even was able to see the time registered on a broken clock on a wall near the patient.

The nurse on duty was quite shocked when her patient revived and reported these events. "I told her what happened," the woman explained in her letter, "but at first she thought I was rambling." The woman went on to say, "This certainly shook her as apparently the lady concerned had a mastoid operation and was just as I described. She was not allowed out of bed, and of course I hadn't been up at all. After several other details, such as the time by the clock on the wall (which had broken down), I convinced her that at least something strange had happened."

Such veridical OBEs are not unusual and have been commonly reported for years. Even though the physical body may seem unconscious during the experience, the percipient's mind is often capable of making accurate and detailed observations from its out-of-body perspective. For example, another one of Green's correspondents had an OBE during a fainting spell at a party: "One moment I felt hot," she explained, "and the next I was looking down at a figure lying face down on the floor. I seemed to be quite high up . . . then I realized the body was mine. I saw my body being picked up, could distinguish clearly individual people and what they were doing, I saw the main lights go on, and then just as suddenly was back in the body again.

". . . I was able to note people's actions and afterward I told them their exact movements, which they confirmed. I was a little embarrassed by having fainted and my partner told me no one had noticed as the main lights in the hall were out; however, I saw the lights go on and someone fetch a chair."

The woman's partner had to admit that these observations were totally correct.

Of course, lying in a hospital bed with pneumonia or fainting at a dance are not exactly the most pleasant experiences in the world. But it is not necessary to undergo such ordeals to have an OBE. Many people experience them quite naturally—that is, while falling asleep, while meditating, through auto-hypnosis, and so on. There are even techniques by which one can allegedly learn to leave the body. This is, of course, the main theme of this book.

Some people experience their out-of-body self as an apparitional double of the physical body and may even see a threadlike cord connecting the two organisms. Others merely experience themselves as a speck or ball of light, or simply float about totally disembodied.

But can just anyone have an out-of-body experience? Or is it a rare psychic ability that only a few gifted individuals ever achieve?

Parapsychological thinking about this issue has changed somewhat over the years. Many researchers of the past felt that OBEs were very rare occurrences, quite outside the range of normal human experience. This view probably arose from the fact that very few people ever spoke about any OBEs they may have had. Since little was known about the experience, most individuals were embarrassed by them. Many feared being labeled crazy by friends and relatives if they began talking about being out of the body.

The idea that the OBE was a rare experience, something only happening to great mystics or powerful psychics, was unfortunately reconfirmed when a few psychics actually *did* start writing about their habitual

disembodied: (apart)

OBEs. Perhaps the first was Hugh Callaway, a British occultist who began publishing accounts of his many OBEs in a series of articles he presented to the *Occult Review,* beginning in 1920. Writing under the pseudonym of Oliver Fox, Callaway wrote not only of his spontaneous OBEs, but also how he trained himself to induce them. At the same time Callaway was traveling light in England, the French mystic Marcel Louis Forhan (or Yram) was experimenting with astral projection and working on his *Le Médecin de l'Ame,* which appeared in English as *Practical Astral Projection.* This book, like Callaway's, was written under a pseudonym. Both these adventurers wrote of classic OBEs, travels to fourth-dimensional worlds, encounters with nonhuman creatures and mystical masters. To those readers who did not merely dismiss Callaway and Yram as romantics pulling the legs of the public, it must have seemed as though only very special and gifted occultists could have out-of-body experiences—or should even try.

In the 1930s, things began to change. The whole idea of astral projection was popularized when Sylvan Muldoon, a sickly youth living in a small town in Wisconsin, began writing his own matter-of-fact accounts of his many OBEs. His first volume, *The Projection of the Astral Body,* appeared in 1929. Written in simple, straightforward language, it lacked the gaudy occult overtones and metaphysics that had saturated his predecessors' writings. Muldoon even advised his readers on how to induce OBEs for themselves. To prove that the OBE was a human potential and not an explicit psychic gift, Muldoon began collecting the accounts of normal, everyday people who had experienced one, or maybe two, OBEs during the course of their daily lives. These accounts, which he published in two lengthy books, were very different from the arcane accounts of Callaway, Forhan, and others. They simply told how the percipients left their bodies momentarily under a variety of conditions, floated about, perhaps even visited a friend or two, and then returned to their bodies none the worse for the experience. The tales were markedly undramatic. Muldoon's work was thus the first serious attempt to demonstrate that the OBE may be a commonly experienced phenomenon attainable by just about anyone—and certainly more common than anyone had hitherto expected.

During the 1960s, Muldoon's point and approaches were expanded by Dr. Robert Crookall, a British geologist with a strong interest in parapsychology, when he, too, started collecting accounts of OBEs experienced by the general public. During the decade from 1961 to 1971, he collected and published some 750 such cases.

So it now seems that the OBE is at least as common as many other garden-variety psychic experiences, such as telepathic "hunches," precognitive dreams, and other forms of extrasensory phenomena that so many of us experience now and then. But just how common OBEs seem to occur came to light only when a handful of researchers began polling the general public about the experience. They were in for a shock.

Dr. Hornell Hart, a sociologist at Duke University in North Carolina, conducted the first such survey in the early 1950s and published his results in 1954. He asked 155 Duke students about the OBE and found that 27 percent of them had undergone at least one such incident sometime during their lives. During the 1960s, Celia Green conducted similar surveys in England. She polled 115 students at Southhampton University; 19 percent admitted having personal experience with the OBE. Green learned that Oxford students were even more familiar with the OBE. When 380 students were similarly questioned, a whopping 34 percent began talking about their projection experiences. Studies conducted during the past few years have borne out the results of these surveys. Dr. Susan Blackmore at the University of Surrey in England found that 11 percent of the 132 students she polled in 1978 had experienced at least one OBE; while Dr. Erlandur Haraldsson and his colleagues in Iceland learned that 8 percent of some 902 adults polled in their homeland admitted to having had such experiences. Dr. John Palmer of the University of Virginia in Charlottesville sent out questionnaires asking the public about any psychic experiences they may have had. Of the 268 students who returned the questionnaires, 25 percent reported OBEs; 14 percent of the 354 adults who filled out the form also admitted having them. A more recent survey was published in 1980 by Dr. Harvey Irwin at the University of New England in Australia. He questioned 177 students about any possible OBEs they may have had, and some 20 percent answered affirmatively.

If we add up all these data and draw a natural implication, it appears that roughly one out of every five people will undergo an OBE at some time during his or her lifetime. This is an extraordinary number!

These statistics contain both implications *and* limitations, of course. They certainly indicate that the OBE is not a rare occult experience. It seems to be common, can occur under a variety of conditions, and does not seem to be as exotic as many of the older occult writers made it appear. On the other hand, these data do not prove that *anyone* can have an OBE, that the ability to leave the body can be nurtured or learned, or that the OBE is unrelated to the possession of psychic ability in general. Since we have no idea how widespread psychic ability is dispersed among the general public, whether the OBE is a normal human potential—as opposed to a particular psychic talent—is a moot point.

However, some new evidence collected by researchers in the United States has done much to show that the OBE probably *is* a human potential, not a talent or hereditary gift. This view comes from two totally different lines of evidence.

The first is an outgrowth of a lengthy and detailed research project undertaken by a team of psychiatrists and psychologists in Kansas. Dr. Glen Gabbard of the Menninger Foundation in Topeka, Dr. Stewart Twemlow of the Topeka V.A. Medical Center, and Dr. Fowler Jones of the University of Kansas Medical Center became interested in the OBE in the late 1970s and began collecting accounts from people who had experienced it. They also began studying the reporters themselves, and presented their first batch of findings at the annual convention of the American Psychiatric Association in May 1980 in San Francisco.

The three researchers reported on several different phases of their work, including how they attempted to map out the characteristics of the OBE, how they tried to determine if a person capable of experiencing this phenomenon is psychologically different from most other people, and whether the OBE can be explained psychiatrically. They received a variety of answers to these questions, but the data in general indicate that the OBE is a widespread human potential that *anyone* is capable of experiencing.

The researchers explained that their research began in February 1976 when Dr. Twemlow was interviewed about his interest in the out-of-body experience for the *National Enquirer.* As part of the interview, the psychiatrist asked any readers who had experienced the OBE to write to him. He received 1,500 letters in response, and 700 of his correspondents described rather typical OBEs. For instance, one government employee wrote to Twemlow about an OBE he had when he was approximately 10 years old.

"I was living together with my older brother at my uncle's house, a major in the U.S. Army Medical Corps," he wrote. "One day I was reclined on my bed quite awake and was looking at the ceiling beams of the old Spanish building where the living quarters were located. I was saying to myself many questions such as what was I doing there and who was I. All of a sudden I got up from the bed and started walking toward the next room. At that moment I felt a strange sensation in me; it was a sensation of weightlessness and a strange mix of a sense of a feeling of joy. I turned back in my steps in order to go back to bed when, to my big surprise, I saw myself reclined on the bed. This surprising experience at that very small age gave me the kind of a jerk which, so to say, shook me back to my body."

Dr. Twemlow was not satisfied merely with these raw cases. He subsequently contacted each of his correspondents by mail, asked them to complete various questionnaires and psychological profiles, and analyzed the results. By using these procedures, he was able to collect and analyze some 339 cases of out-of-body travel. This data base, he told his colleagues at the A.P.A. meeting, allowed him to determine what factors seem to precipitate OBEs, what characteristics they share, and what kind of people tend to have them or at least report them.

The results of Twemlow's initial survey closely resembled what many previous researchers have discovered. Most of his correspondents (79 percent) were in a calm and relaxed state when they had their spontaneous astral flights, while his other correspondents had their experiences during childbirth, as a result of anesthesia, or during bouts of extreme pain. He was also able to determine that people who have practiced meditation seem particularly prone to spontaneous OBEs. The fact that 79 percent of these respondents were under no crisis, threat, or illness at the time indicates that the OBE may well be a very normal human experience and not something catalyzed under unusual—or life-threatening—circumstances. The *types* of experiences his informants apparently underwent were also fairly representative of the OBE in general. Most of them told how they initially heard odd roaring sounds in their ears before undergoing their OBEs, felt themselves "leaving their bodies" and seeing them left behind, passed through walls as they projected, and experienced other near-legendary aspects of out-of-body travel.

What particularly struck the researchers, however, was the general naivety of their correspondents about the OBE. "It was significant that approximately one-third of the sample had not expected in any way to have such an experience," the Kansas psychiatrists reported as part of their

A.P.A. presentations, "and did not admit . . . expecting or even knowing about such experiences."

And how did these informants react to their OBEs? Most of them loved them!

The psychiatrists reported that a whopping 85 percent of those who took part in the survey described the experience as pleasant and over half of them described it as "joyful." This finding certainly indicates that the OBE is an experience that we should nurture and that will probably bring great satisfaction to our physical and spiritual lives. The experience also seems to have profoundly affected the way in which many of the reporters viewed both life and death. Over two-thirds of them explained that the experience had helped alleviate their fear of death and encouraged their belief in an afterlife. "Fully 43 percent of the subjects considered it to be the greatest thing that had ever happened to them," the psychiatrists told their colleagues. Most of them wanted to try it again. The three researchers were also impressed by the fact that most of those questioned were absolutely certain that they were not dreaming when they had their OBEs.

But does it take a special type of person to undergo an out-of-body experience? This question was a natural one for the psychiatrists to explore. Having been trained in the study of the human personality and mind, the Kansas team soon wondered if a person who has had an OBE, or who is at least capable of experiencing one, is somehow psychologically "different" from most other people. Many parapsychologists who have studied the OBE have wondered the same thing. But the Kansas researchers are the first scientists to actually attempt an empirical exploration of this question.

In light of the overwhelming response to Twemlow's press interview, Jones and Gabbard had no lack of subjects to study. They sent out detailed questionnaires to these individuals in an attempt to find the answers to such questions as: Do people who have OBEs have particularly active imaginations? Are they more hysterical or psychotic than most people? Are they actually better adjusted? It was not difficult to answer these questions after the questionnaires were returned. They were able to collect detailed information from 80 of their correspondents, which answered the questions most concisely. The conclusion? People who have OBEs are just like everyone else! They tend to be fairly well adjusted and otherwise very unexceptional.

Such psychological findings are very important for several reasons.

Chief among these is that psychiatrists have often thought that people who report OBEs are either mentally ill or at least headed in that direction. The pioneering work of Twemlow, Gabbard, and Jones has shown that the OBE is in no way the product of a disturbed mind. It is especially noteworthy to find that most of the subjects turned out to be extremely well adjusted and felt that the OBE was a pleasant nonanxiety-provoking adventure. Being clinicians by training, the Kansas team members are very well aware of the implications that their research holds for the psychiatric community in general. They argued throughout their presentations that the OBE can no longer be considered any form of aberrant experience.

The psychiatrists even devoted one of their three A.P.A. presentations to this very issue, and they surveyed what they had learned about the OBE by comparing it to several anomalous psychological experiences sometimes reported by mental patients. They showed that none of these aberrant mental experiences could subsume the classical OBE. They focused their attention especially on such clinical phenomena as depersonalization, autoscopy, and distortion of body image.

Depersonalization, they explained, does not lead one to feel as though he or she has left the body. It also usually produces a panic reaction in the sufferer and occurs when the person is anxious or psychologically aroused. This is all very different, they point out, from the classical OBE, which is usually a calming and transcending experience. The doctors made a similar case against the idea that the OBE is a form of autoscopy, a relatively rare phenomenon in which the sufferer sees his or her own apparition, usually from the chest up, transparent, and mimicking the moves he or she is making with the physical body. This, too, is all very different from the way OBEs are described. And after surveying the literature on body image distortion, the psychiatrists could find no evidence that specific hallucinations of actually leaving and re-entering the body were a characteristic of this type of experience.

These pertinent issues were raised since the Kansas team were aware that some people, having spontaneously experienced an OBE, might seek out a psychiatrist for help. The result might be disastrous, they warned, if the psychiatrist is unfamiliar with the commonness of the OBE. "Perhaps education as to the nature of the experience and reassurances that it is one that others have shared may be more therapeutic to the person having the out-of-body experience than conventional psychiatric interventions," they told their fellow mental health workers. They even hinted that perhaps such a patient would gain more relief by talking to a yogi than to a psychiatrist!

In summary, then, the work of the Kansas team has shown that: (1) the OBE is an experience widespread among the general public, (2) that it is pleasurable and may even be psychologically advantageous to have one, (3) that it is a normal human experience, and (4) no special type of person is particularly prone to having one. The natural implication of this research is that we all possess the potential for out-of-body travel and to use it in the course of our day-to-day living.

But just because we have the capacity to experience an OBE or two, does that mean we can actually learn to do it at will? This question is tricky and controversial. However, my own feeling is that the answer is yes, and that a sizable amount of experimental evidence supports this view. This is yet a second major line of evidence in support of the "human potential" view of the OBE.

Some of the most pertinent experimental research confirming this view has been that of John Palmer at John F. Kennedy University in Orinda, California. Dr. Palmer began experimentally studying the OBE during the mid-1970s when he was a research associate at the University of Virginia. Palmer has long argued that *if* the OBE is a human potential, it should be possible to induce the experience in volunteer subjects by having them follow certain "training" procedures. He was impressed by the fact that many of those very special people who can voluntarily undergo OBEs begin by relaxing, entering into an OBE-conducive state of altered consciousness, and then imagine themselves leaving the body as a prelude to inducing the experience. So the young psychologist began training people in these procedures. His project led to some curious successes.

Dr. Palmer conducted his first experiment at the University of Virginia by testing 60 volunteer students who claimed no particular psychic ability. He met with the students individually, briefed them about the ability to develop the OBE, then recruited them for the experiment. The idea behind the initial meeting was to encourage the students to believe that they *could* induce the experience by following certain training procedures. Each subject was then taken to a lab room where he or she was shown a table upon which a picture was to be placed during the upcoming test. The student was asked to orient him- or herself to the room, since he or she would later be asked to journey there while out-of-body. The volunteer was then taken to another room, placed in a chair, and taught how to relax completely by progressively tensing and releasing each muscle group of the body. Then the volunteer was subjected to a state of mild disorientation. A monotonous sine-wave tone was played into the subject's ears through headphones, while he or she was made to stare into a rotating spiral vortex disc. The student was then asked to imagine him- or herself leaving the body and entering into the spiral.

If the subject succeeded in inducing an OBE, he or she was then asked to visit the adjoining lab room and take a look at a picture that had been placed on the table. This part of the test was designed to "prove" that the volunteer actually had been out of body.

This technique for inducing OBEs in the volunteers was quite successful. When asked if, at any time during the experiment, it seemed that they were *literally* out of the body, some 42 percent of the subjects answered affirmatively. Unfortunately however, few of them were successful in correctly describing the target picture. This was particularly odd, since many of the subjects felt that they *had* seen it.

Palmer soon replicated his experiment by testing 40 additional subjects. Also conducted at the University of Virginia, this research project was designed along the lines of the first experiment, but several refinements were introduced. The subjects for this test were first relaxed through the use of progressive muscle relaxation, but Palmer did away with the spiral disc. Instead, he taped halved ping-pong balls over the students' eyes and had them stare into a red light. "White noise" was played into their ears through headphones. This setting, technically called "ganzfeld [homogeneous field] stimulation," is known to produce slight disorientation and daydreamlike imagery. Palmer felt that this state of sensory isolation might be more powerful than the spiral disc in helping his subjects feel as if they were "leaving the body." As in his first experiment, he also instructed his volunteers to "visit" an adjoining room and see what picture had been placed there on a table.

As an added part of the experiment, however, Dr. Palmer instructed only 20 of his subjects actually to leave the body during the test. The others were merely asked to "image" about the picture in the next room. This precaution was taken to discover the relative roles that out-of-body travel and "normal" ESP might play in the experiment.

The results of this test were more straightforward than Palmer obtained during his first experiment. No fewer than 13 out of the 20 subjects who were specifically *told* to leave their bodies during the ganzfeld stimulation reported OBEs. However, four of the "control" group reported spontaneous OBEs. The subjects who reported the OBEs tended to describe the target picture with some degree of sucess and more consistently than did the other volunteers. This would, of course, indicate that during the test these people really had been able to leave their bodies and visit the next room.

Dr. Palmer conducted yet a third experiment in which he used a vibrating chair during the induction procedures, along with ganzfeld stimulation. Since many people who have had OBEs report that their bodies vibrated as though an electrical current were being passed through them, Palmer thought that producing this sensation artificially might help induce the experience. He was right. During the upcoming experiments, he tested 40 subjects with this new technique, and nearly half of them reported OBEs.

Now it could be argued that Palmer's subjects were merely *imagining* that they had left their bodies and did not really experience classic OBEs. However, this theory cannot explain all the results. Some of the subjects reported experiences virtually indistinguishable from the types of spontaneous OBEs that people report as a result of accident or when nearing sleep.

For instance, one subject described how he suddenly became aware of being out-of-body. "At first during the relaxation," he told Palmer, "I felt like a rush of . . . excitement, sort of, and I felt completely detached from everything. Then when I was supposed to be trying to leave my body, my mind became very alert and analytical and I felt in a box sort of inside a dead body. This continued the whole way through the experiment, and when it was over I felt a big come-down when the tape clicked off. I felt sort of the whole way through also, like I could see my whole body down beneath me in the chair, and once I felt like my mind was in a yellow glow right above my eyes close to my head and it was me, but I could also see it; and I tried to imagine the room with myself in it and I felt like I was very wide awake seeing the room. And there is an impression of a picture of blue-green and bright reddish-brown, but that could be a picture I just had in my mind."

Other subjects reported initial sensations of leaving the body, reminiscent of the way some people describe the onset of spontaneous OBEs. For instance, one of Palmer's students said that ". . . I had a sense of sliding out of the back of the chair. I seemed to be still in my body, but there was a definite sense of motion of two or three feet back. In a second I just seemed to raise up a bit—a floating sense—like in a tub of water."

Partially as a result of his project, Dr. Palmer has come to several conclusions about the nature of the OBE. He believes that it is indeed possible to induce the experience, and that several states of altered attention, such as sensory isolation and relaxation, seem related to it. He also considers that certain psychological factors help people to experience the state. Palmer was struck by the fact that those subjects who were especially *told* to have or expect an OBE as a result of the induction procedures had them more frequently than subjects who were not so instructed. (This finding was quite clear in his second major experiment.) This has led Palmer to conclude that *psychological expectation is a key factor in helping people to induce OBEs*. In other words, if you believe a certain technique will work, it probably will.

But if the OBE *is* a potential, why doesn't everyone experience the phenomenon? Why didn't *all* of Palmer's subjects experience OBEs? And, as pointed out at the beginning of this chapter, why is only one person in five likely to undergo this adventure during his or her lifetime? There must be some hidden factor that determines who will, and who will not, find him- or herself leaving the body at some point. Even the procedures Palmer worked out at the University of Virginia induced OBEs in only about half the subjects he tested. Why did the others fail?

One possible solution to this puzzle came to light in August 1978 when Palmer addressed a convention of parapsychologists at Washington University in St. Louis. He reported that toward the end of his University of Virginia project, he had started monitoring the brain waves of his volunteers, hoping to determine if any brain-wave changes occur when a person experiences an OBE. Palmer made a surprising discovery: Subjects whose brain-wave patterns showed an abundance of theta waves while they were preparing for the experiment invariably reported OBEs during the forthcoming test. Palmer explained that during the course of his work, he came across three subjects who showed over 30 percent theta in their resting parietal EEGs. All three subsequently had OBEs as a result of his induction procedures.

This was too much of a coincidence to overlook. But just what is so special about theta waves?

Theta waves are perhaps the most mysterious of the brain's rhythms.

We know that the brain constantly produces small electrical pulsations, which can be monitored by placing electrodes on the scalp. The resulting tracings are then graphed out by an electroencephalograph. These waves are grouped into four categories. The most predominate is the *beta* wave, which registers between 14-30 cycles per second and accompanies any sort of intellectual activity such as problem-solving. When we relax and clear our minds, our brain waves slow down to between 8-12 cycles; these are called *alpha* waves. *Delta* waves are even lower, between 1/2-3 cycles, and usually appear during deep sleep; they indicate brain pathology when they occur in a waking EEG. The uncommon *theta* waves, which come between alpha and delta waves at 4-7 cycles, seem to manifest when a person is involved in a deep alteration of consciousness. Intense creative exercises or yogic meditation seem to induce them, and they also occur when an individual attempts to create intense mental imagery or when deliberately inducing an altered state of consciousness.

Palmer's discovery indicates that a naturally relaxed and meditative individual may be particularly prone to having OBEs. It may be that those with a natural ability to clear their minds and alter their attention away from the outside world might also possess the ability to leave the body.

The possible discovery of a link between theta waves and the OBE also holds out a very special promise to people who wish to induce the experience. It is possible to learn how to generate theta waves through biofeedback, and nurturing such a capability may lead to the development of OBE skills. Dr. Elmer Green has been studying biofeedback techniques for several years in Topeka, Kansas, at the Menninger Foundation, an institute devoted solely to psychological research. He has had singular success in teaching people to control their brain waves, including theta waves. In fact, Green has publicly stated that people who develop control over theta waves start having psychic experiences as a result. Perhaps this ties in with Palmer's findings.

The discovery that the OBE may be related to specific brain-wave rhythms is one of the most exciting new avenues of potential research on the subject. As Palmer reported during his Washington University presentation, ". . . if this relationship should bear out in future research, it may be possible to develop biofeedback techniques to either facilitate OBEs or . . . to prevent their spontaneous occurrence in persons who wish to be rid of them." Future research is obviously needed to resolve the issue.

It may seem as though these various findings and surveys are a mishmash of unrelated data, but such is not the case. A careful scrutiny of these recent explorations into the phenomenon of the OBE reveals several mutually consistent discoveries. In summing up, one might say that no particular type of person is especially prone to having OBEs and that specific "induction" techniques can aid the individual who wishes to undergo one. Moreover, the chances of having an OBE are increased if one can learn to control the electrical pulsations of the brain.

Therefore, it appears that inducing OBEs is a skill just about anyone can learn, rather than being an inherited talent or a God-given ability.

Now the question naturally arises whether one should really try to deliberately self-induce OBEs. Are there dangers to astral projection? Or are there any particular benefits to be attained through the practice? My own thinking has changed over the years on this issue.

The old occult school of thought was that out-of-body travel could be dangerous. This view, especially promoted by Hugh Callaway, fits in with his beliefs that astral travel is limited to the special few (such as himself) who are well along the often treacherous path of spiritual enlightenment. In one of his *Occult Review* pieces, he wrote that ". . . though I *do* know that some of the symptoms [of leaving the body] are painful and extremely unpleasant, I have no evidence that they are really as dangerous as they feel or injurious to the health of the experimenter." Callaway suggested nonetheless that "nervous" people and those with weak hearts should stay clear of experimenting with astral projection. He also held out the possibility that heart failure, insanity, cerebral hemorrhage, injurious effects on returning to the body, and obsession by discarnate beings result from the practice. However, it is important to note that Callaway based his views on the occult beliefs common in his day and culture and had no actual evidence that any of these horrible catastrophes awaited the out-of-body voyager.* A case *was* reported in the press some years ago of a youth found dead in his room after experimenting with out-of-body travel. His friends claimed that he had voluntarily left his body—permanently. But an autopsy revealed a more material cause of his death; he died of a drug overdose.

---

*It is only fair to note, however, that in the 1932 book, The Maniac, the authoress E. Thelmar claimed that a psychotic episode she lived through was a result of her astral projections. The book is fascinating but totally unique in the literature. The OBEs she reported could have been unrelated to her temporary psychosis, or may have only catalyzed a pre-existing condition.

When I began my own experimentation with astral projection as a teenager, I was greatly influenced by the writings of such grand masters as Callaway, Forhan, and Muldoon, and unquestioningly abided by their dictums that mind travel could be fraught with all sorts of physical, mental, and spiritual dangers. I had indeed experienced some unpleasant side effects from my own experiences. So when I first began describing various techniques for inducing the out-of-body state (in an article for *Fate* magazine in 1973), I said that "astral projection is actually dangerous for very basic physiological and psychological reasons." I argued that experimenting with out-of-body travel could be injurious to the body's normal homeostatic functions. I was especially concerned about how these induction techniques could affect oxygen supply to the brain, the normal regulation of the heartbeat, and so on.

Looking back on my experiences, about which I will speak in more detail later, I think my attitude was rather reactionary and naive. Astral projection is not an "occult" experience that only self-selected initiates should nurture for the purpose of spiritual advancement. It is a normal, healthy experience that anyone—doctor, lawyer, or candlestick maker—has the capacity to undergo. And since it is so normal, it is very unlikely that there are any dangers inherent in the practice. Remember that the Kansas team found that the overwhelming majority of those polled reported their OBEs as enjoyable; indeed, many wanted to have more such experiences. Some people *were* scared by their sudden release from the body, but there is a huge difference between an event *experienced* as frightening and one that is objectively dangerous. In most cases, the fright was a psychological reaction to the OBE, not to any inherent danger. Fright reactions are usually experienced by people with no knowledge of the OBE and who are, therefore, mentally unprepared for undergoing one.

During my own first OBEs, I, too, was frightened by the paralysis that often accompanied the releases, by the way my body felt burning hot while I tried to induce them, by the way my heart raced when I returned to the body, and by some other minor side effects. But as I grew more accustomed to the OB state, these experiences receded to the background. Either they no longer manifested when I underwent the OBE, or I simply did not notice them any longer. It is my own retrospective feeling that many of these side effects are actually caused by the mind's (and body's) resistance to the experience; they may not be inherent to the experience itself.

It is now fairly well known that any procedure that places the mind in a new relationship to the body will have certain side effects for a limited number of people. Even simple meditation can be unpleasant at first. Some individuals go through a period of unpleasant body sensations, tics, and anxiety when they begin meditation. This is not common, but it is perfectly normal. This "settling down" phase usually ceases in time. Zen students are even warned that they may go through a period of unpleasant mental imagery as they begin meditation practices. They are advised to simply ignore the images, which will no doubt go away in time. The OBE may be no different in this respect. The mind and body may react unpleasantly at first, but there is no real reason to believe that these side effects are in any way harmful. In my own case, they totally ceased during the first year of my experimentation.

Of course, one of the most common questions about the experience is whether someone can get "locked" out of the body while mind traveling. The answer seems to be no. All of the great astral projectors of the past experimented with prolonging the out-of-body state. Most deliberately attempted to remain out of the body even after they intuitively felt that it was time to return. In just about every instance, they found themselves returning to the body involuntarily. It would seem that the body and mind have their own regulations about how long an OBE can last—rules that even willful volition cannot override.

So, all in all, it does not seem that anyone need be overly concerned about the often-touted dangers of astral projection. True dangers probably do not exist. Even the unpleasant side effects probably only occur infrequently. Why else would so many one-timers express the desire to have another crack at it?

In my own estimation, the OBE is a gratifying experience that holds many lessons for us. It demonstrates that the mind is an entity in its own right, something distinct from the brain and body. I have never met anyone who has had an OBE who is still a materialist. The experience also helps us to gain a greater totality of the universe than we can perceive while locked in the confines of the physical body. OBEs can also help one overcome the fear of death. To some, they are the literal demonstration of personal immortality. Other benefits to the OBE will be discussed at the conclusion of this book.

I have certainly learned much from my own OBEs. I think anybody who eventually achieves the ability will say the same.

REFERENCES

Crookall, Robert. *The Study and Practice of Astral Projection.* London: Aquarian Press, 1961.

———. *More Astral Projections.* London: Aquarian Press, 1964.

———. *Casebook of Astral Projection.* Secaucus, N.J.: University Books, 1972.

Fox, Oliver. *Astral Projection.* New Hyde Park, N.Y.: University Books, 1962 (Reprint).

Green, Celia. *Out-of-the-Body Experiences.* Oxford, England: Institute of Psychophysical Research, 1968.

Green, Elmer, and Green, Alyce. *Beyond Biofeedback.* New York: Delacorte, 1977.

Muldoon, Sylvan. *The Case for Astral Projection.* Chicago: Aries Press, 1946.

Muldoon, Sylvan and Carrington, Hereward. *The Projection of the Astral Body.* London: Rider, 1929.

———. *The Phenomena of Astral Projection.* London: Rider, 1951.

Palmer, John. ESP and out-of-body experiences: EEG correlates. In *Research in Parapsychology-1978.* Metuchen, N.J.: Scarecrow Press, 1979.

Palmer, John, and Lieberman, R. The influence of psychological set on ESP and out-of-body experiences. *Journal of the American Society for Psychical Research,* 1975, *69,* 193-213.

———. ESP and out-of-body experiences: A further study. In *Research in Parapsychology-1975.* Metuchen, N.J.: Scarecrow Press, 1976.

Palmer, John, and Vasser, C. ESP and out-of-body experiences: An exploratory study. *Journal of the American Society for Psychical Research,* 1974, *68,* 257-80.

Rogo, D. Scott. Astral projection a risky practice? *Fate,* May, 1973.

Twemlow, Stuart W.; Gabbard, Glen O.; Jones, Fowler C. The out-of-body experience. I: Phenomenology; II: Psychological profile; III: Differential diagnosis. Set of three papers delivered at the 1980 convention of the American Psychiatric Association.

Yram. *Practical Astral Projection.* London: Rider, n.d.

chapter two
Projection Through Dynamic Concentration

Many techniques traditionally used to induce the out-of-body experience focus on relaxation, entering a sleeplike state, auto-hypnosis, or the induction of similar "twilight zone" states of consciousness. Formal induction procedures based on these practices are outlined in many of the following chapters. But few people realize that one of the first empirically derived methods for inducing OBEs was much more dynamic and volitional. The key was the use of directly focused concentration. This technique was first developed by French researchers around the turn of the twentieth century, although their research and procedures are barely remembered today.

BACKGROUND

The French psychical researchers of the nineteenth century were a product of a rich heritage of French and German occultism. Basing their views on the writings of Franz Anton Mesmer and his followers (who discovered the precursor of modern hypnosis), these investigators believed that the human body contained a cosmic or psychic "fluid." Partially material and partially immaterial at the same time, this mysterious fluid could be exteriorized from the body. A psychic, it was believed, could exteriorize this invisible substance at will and through it, produce psychic phenomena, such as moving an object without touching it. The fluid could even be made to permeate a building, which would subsequently become haunted. In many respects, the psychic fluid of the occultists is similar to what Soviet parapsychologists today call "bioplasma."

These French scholars were also fascinated by a phenomenon known to the mesmerists as "traveling clairvoyance." Many researchers of the day believed that a hypnotized subject could be told to send his or her mind to a distant location and see what was happening there. Impressive evidence was collected by a number of these researchers documenting the existence of this wondrous phenomenon. (One well-known case concerns a well-known researcher in France who asked his young subject to locate his father and follow him wherever he went. The lad found his father walking the streets across town and entering a house of questionable repute. On checking the accuracy of the report, the subject's father admitted that the boy's observations were correct—and then begged the experimenter never to conduct such an experiment again!)

The natural outgrowth of these observations was the belief that the body consisted of not only a physical organism, but a "fluidic" double that could be exteriorized and travel about as a disembodied apparition, taking the human consciousness along with it. (Notice again how similar this is to the belief of many Soviet researchers that we each house a semi-material "bioplasmic body" within us.) Soon many French psychic investigators were designing tests to prove the double's existence.

The most systematic work along these lines was conducted by Hector Durville, a hypnotist and general secretary of the Magnetic Society in France. A keenly critical and innovative researcher, he did much to demonstrate objectively the existence of the fluidic double, and he began publishing his findings in a series of detailed reports and papers that first appeared in 1908. They are fascinating to read even today.

Most of his experiments were conducted in Durville's own home. For one series of tests, he and a colleague hypnotized a female psychic. An observer was placed in another part of the house. The experimenters "sent" their subject's double into the distant room and instructed it to either touch, hit, or pull at the observer. These trials were invariably successful. The observer, who had no idea what the subject's double would be requested to do, often felt blows, touches, or pulls by invisible hands. The phantom double was even visible to some of the people whom Durville used as witnesses. They usually described it as a whitish apparitional figure and saw an odd cordlike extension protruding from its head or stomach (leading back to the subject's physical body).

Durville's most intriguing discovery was that many people, who did not otherwise consider themselves psychic, could often perceive even the *invisible* presence of the double. He conducted several tests during which the observer sat in one room and tried to "guess" when colleagues were sending their subject's phantom to him or her.

"When the phantom approached the spectators," wrote Durville in a 1908 summary of his work, "nine out of ten of them become aware of its presence by a feeling of coolness which comes over them and which disappears soon after it has gone away again. Some perceive distinctly a sort of breath, which somewhat resembles that felt when standing near an electrostatic machine in operation. When the phantom has stood for six or eight minutes near persons placed at one end of my study, it seems to them that that part of the room has become sensibly colder. There are a few persons who do not perceive this sensation of coolness, but who receive other impressions. Thus, on the approach of the phantom, especially when it has stood before him for 40 or 50 seconds, [one subject] feels a moisture in his hands, and especially at the ends of his fingers. If the phantom remains longer, this moisture spreads to the upper part of his body. Others feel a slight trembling, a sort of shivering, which is curious without being disagreeable."

The French experimenter later succeeded in having the fluidic double carry out physical—that is, telekinetic—displays. The liberated double could produce raps by knocking its "hand" on a table, close a half open door, and so on.

For example, below is the complete protocol for one such experiment held in Durville's study. Two witnesses, a M. Dubois and another colleague, were present. The subject was placed in hypnosis and then the double was released through suggestion.

I caused the double to be projected, and when it seemed sufficiently condensed I asked it, when it could, to strike more blows on the table. After two or three minutes we heard some crackings in the table, which no one was touching, then two light blows were distinctly heard, as though struck with the tip of a finger. I asked the phantom to give two more raps. I had scarcely expressed this desire when two blows similar to the former ones were heard. I allowed the subject to rest for a few moments, then I asked the phantom to give three more raps. Crackings were heard in the table and immediately afterwards three blows similar to the former ones were distinctly heard.

At this moment someone rang at the door. The subject became agitated, and I found that the phantom was no longer near the table, nor in the armchair placed for it on the subject's left. I asked the subject where the phantom was. "It has gone to see who is at the door," was the reply. I asked who it was that had come to disturb us, and if we should open the door. "It is a man," she said, "who has come to see you; you can open the door." I asked M. Dubois to go and open the door for the visitor, who was about to go away. It was Dr. Ridet, who came to bring me a manuscript. He was shown into the study where the experiments were taking place.

The phantom had returned to the chair, but was disorganized, and the subject was enervated. I calmed her, and then tried to condense the phantom. When this appeared to be sufficiently accomplished, I asked it to approach the table and give two raps. After two or three minutes, crackings were heard in the table, and then three raps were heard, as though struck with the fleshy part of the fingers of the open hand.

The subject was enervated and afflicted by the presence of the new witness, with whom she was not acquainted. Fearing a nervous attack, I awoke her gradually, with the usual precautions. Though somewhat fatigued, she was in good physical and mental condition.

No doubt Durville's greatest achievement was photographing the double of one of his subjects. He obtained two such magnesium plate photographs that show a vaguely human form, white but opaque.

Another French researcher of this same period was Dr. Charles Lancelin, a physician and a keen student of occultism and psychical research. He shared Durville's concepts about the fluidic double and even worked with some of his colleague's subjects. Lancelin, however, believed that the projection of the human phantom could be brought under volitional control. Because he did not feel that hypnosis was essential to its exteriorization, he began systematic research on the self-induction of the phantom double.

Lancelin eventually produced a 559-page volume, *Methodes de Dédoublement Personnel* in which he reported his research, theories, and techniques for astral projection. The book also discussed many of the techniques taught within the oral traditions of France's many occult circles, and their publication caused quite a sensation.

THE TECHNIQUE

Lancelin felt that astral projection was both a science and an art, and that many a priori conditions must be met before one could learn to leave the body. First of all, one must have the correct "temperament" for the experiments. Temperament, according to Lancelin, might be defined as a "physiological state produced by the predominance of an element, organ or system in the human body." A person with a nervous temperament was considered the best suited for self-inducing OBEs. Today we might say that a person with a nervous temperament is someone who is suggestible, prone to hypnosis, easily absorbed by nature or in creative endeavors, keenly aware of information cued to him or her from the environment, sensitive to the people around him or her, and especially to information picked up through various modes of nonverbal communication. Although the term *neurotic* would not be an apt translation of what Lancelin meant by a nervous temperament, perhaps "highly sensitive and reactive to people and the physical environment" might do the phrase more justice.

The second criteria for a successful essay into the weird domains of astral travel is the subject's health. He or she should be in good health, of calm emotion, and of placid mind. The subject must also have an iron-clad will, whose use is the key to Lancelin's teaching. One must be able to strengthen the will until the act of willing becomes an unconscious process as well as a conscious one. This means that to produce an OBE, the subject must learn how to "will" something to happen with such focused concentration that no intervening thoughts can usurp the willed-upon desire from its pre-eminence in the consciousness. After a while, this process of "willing" will become unconscious—that is, the willed-upon action and desire will stay in mind even when the subject is no longer consciously involved in the act of willing.

This may sound very abstract, but it really is not. Let me cite an example of this type of willing. Once I was visiting with a New York psychic who had successfully demonstrated the ability to move small objects with her mind. She had even been filmed producing these effects; very fine motion pictures were taken of her moving a small vial across a countertop in her kitchen. When I asked her how she did it, she explained that it was a matter of will. She focused on the object she wanted to affect and with all her might willed it to move. This process of willing went on until she lost all awareness of her physical surroundings, and she began to "merge" with the object. At that point, only she and it existed, and she could move it just as if it were an extension of her own body. This is what Lancelin meant by dynamic willing.

Hereward Carrington, a serious student of astral projection, and a psychical researcher of some note before his death in Los Angeles in 1958, was also one of the few scholars familiar with Lancelin's work. He presented the first summary of it in English in 1919 and offered some specific exercises for learning how to dynamize the will consciously.

"The first thing to do then," he suggested, "to ensure the success of our 'astral projection,' is to *dynamize the will*—to hyperdynamize it, in fact, so that it is overcharged, and capable of bursting out, like champagne, when the cork is removed. There are various methods of doing this. One of the simplest is to repeat to oneself many times just before dropping off to sleep, "I have will—I have energy!" This must be kept up until sleep actually supervenes, and memory is lost. Then one may think of the next day's work clearly, in detail, and make up one's mind not to deviate therefrom, even under great pressure and temptation. This will give the subconscious will a force that nothing else can equal."

But what about Lancelin's concept of unconscious willing? This might best be explained by an analogy. Have you ever had a problem, such as being caught short of cash with nowhere to turn, that bothered you so much that you found yourself constantly preoccupied with it? You thought about it, replaying the problem in your mind over and over until it haunted you day and night. Just about everyone has gone through such an ordeal. You probably found yourself thinking about the problem at unexpected moments. At some point you might have been working or playing when you gradually realized that, in the back of your mind, you had been thinking about the problem and how to solve it. This is what Lancelin meant by unconscious willing.

It is interesting that this process is very similar to certain procedures taught in traditional magic. The initiate is told to hold a desire in mind so strongly and with such focus that eventually the unconscious mind takes over control of the willing and causes the desired event to occur through occult means. Before specifically attempting astral projection, the desire and preoccupation to induce it should already have been made at this level.

This type of focused, unidirectional willing is really not as arcane as it might sound. It is very similar to the Christian concept of dynamic prayer—that through fervent desire and faith, changes in the world will occur through the intermediacy of God. According to occult belief, these changes can occur *directly* through the action of the will. Nonetheless, the techniques of dynamic willing and concentrated prayer are really very much the same. The desire must become all-consuming on all levels of the mind.

These instructions are actually training exercises at which the student should become adept before the actual attempt to astral project is made. After one has successfully learned the techniques of dynamic willing, the second phase of the program—the process of "loosening" the double from the physical body—may begin. Here is how it is done:

Sit down in a comfortable chair, or lie in bed, and go over your entire body in thought. Focus on each inch of the body with all your might and will that the double detach itself at that point. Try to feel, not merely imagine, the human double detaching at each point. After completing this procedure, focus all your mental energy on the solar plexus or the forehead and will that your mind and double release from the body. You cannot just want it to happen; you must exercise an almost exhausting effort of will.

Even if you do not have a classic OBE at this time, it might be a good idea to imagine that you *have* actually left the body. Imagine yourself liberated from the body and travel about your room. Notice everything in detail. You might find that you are more "out" than you believe.

To validate the experience of exteriorization, Lancelin suggested a cooperative effort with a friend. Go through the procedure outlined above, then will yourself to your friend's home or room, and see if he or she actually sees you. Someone who is somewhat psychic might be the best recruit. The tip here is to hold the image of your friend in mind at all times while willing yourself to leave the body. Envision the friend's face at the end of a tunnel and project yourself down through it and to his or her home. While trying to induce this OBE, have your friend simultaneously focus his or her concentration on you. This might help draw you to the person.

Apart from the purely psychological aspects of the Lancelin techniques, certain atmospheric and situational factors may also contribute to the success or failure of your experiments. For instance:

1. *Atmospheric conditions should be dry and clear, and barometric conditions high.*
2. *Do not try to induce OBEs when the atmosphere is electrically charged. It is not wise to try to project during thunderstorms.*
3. *The temperature should be mild to warm, not less than 20 degrees below the normal temperature of the human body.*
4. *When attempting to induce an OBE, wear only loose clothing or none at all.*
5. *Make the attempts in darkness or in only very dim light.*
6. *Make the projection while you are alone.*
7. *Ensure dead silence before the experiment begins, since any sudden or distracting noise might catch your attention and ruin your concentration.*
8. *Conduct the trials late at night when sleep is most likely to supervene.*
9. *It is best to sit or lie down comfortably. For optimal results, lie either on the right side or on the back. You should not lie on your left side.*

According to Lancelin, astral projection is a difficult matter that one should approach slowly and cautiously. It was his belief that the out-of-body experience could be used to explore unseen dimensions of time and space and that one should be both mentally and spiritually prepared for the experience. He basically took an occultist view of the OBE, a view that—as suggested in the first chapter—may not be correct. However, there is no doubt that Lancelin's techniques were the most advanced of his day and were based on the writings and practices of many of France's greatest occultists. His own work had verified many of these techniques, and they should be taken seriously.

COMMENTS

The techniques and prerequisite conditions discussed earlier may strike the reader as rather arbitrary, but one must remember that Lancelin based his views on years of empirical observations and experimentations. His *magnum opus* has never appeared in English. Carrington's summary hardly does it justice; so it is impossible to explain the rationale and evidence that the French researcher marshaled for his various views and suggestions. Lancelin's research is probably *the* most authoritative empirically derived system for the willful projection of the double. It is, therefore, a pity that it is so little known in the United States or to students of astral projection in general.

My own respect for Lancelin's research has grown considerably over the years, much of it based on my own experiences and experiments in the art of out-of-body travel. As stated in the introduction, through systematic experimentation, I began having OBEs in 1965. They were relatively frequent from 1965 to 1967, during which time I gained some control over them. In thinking about them in retrospect, many of the conditions surrounding my OBEs were consistent with Lancelin's views. For instance, they usually occurred under those conditions that Lancelin believed to favor astral projection—during warm weather, when I was nearing sleep, at times of utter stillness, and so on. My projections also occurred when I was either on my back or my right side. In fact, I found that I could abort an incipient OBE by flipping onto my left side. Just why this should be so, I do not know, but it is uncannily consistent with what Lancelin discovered.

The comments he made about atmospheric conditions are also intriguing. When I traveled to Durham, North Carolina, in 1973 to work at the Psychical Research Foundation, I met and spent six weeks working with S. Keith Harary (called Blue), a Duke University undergraduate who could induce OBEs at will. During those weeks, Blue demonstrated his ability to leave the body, travel to distant locations, "see" what was going on there, make animals react to his presence, and even cause his apparition to appear on rare occasions. (The whole story of Harary's abilities is told in Chapter 3). However, Blue was adamant about one thing. He would not project during thunderstorms or when such a storm was threatening. He felt that the electrical buildup in the atmosphere hampered his abilities and disoriented him. He also disliked approaching any kind of powerlines during his projections. Sometimes, he told me, he would get "caught" by the lines and become stuck to them.

I do not think these were imaginary claims. On at least one occasion, we tested Blue when a storm was approaching. He had requested a postponement, but we had encouraged him to go through with the test. He was taken to Duke University Hospital, placed in a sealed booth, and asked to project to the P.R.F. lab. Once there he was to look at a display we had arranged for him and report back on what he saw. (The display consisted of several lab items placed on a large drum.) Blue predicted that he would fail because of the storm, and he was right. Yet the previous week he had performed magnificently on the same task.

Later during my stay in Durham, I had the chance to analyze several cases of spontaneous OBEs sent to the lab by people who had heard of our research. One woman described how she had approached some powerlines during one of her OBEs, had become stuck to them, and had to travel down them before ultimately breaking loose. The case was a fascinating parallel to what Blue had told us. It may well be, as Lancelin suggested, that OBEs and electricity just don't mix.

By far, however, Lancelin's greatest contribution to the study of astral projection was his emphasis on the contribution that dynamic willing—on both conscious and unconscious levels—plays during the self-induction of the OBE. Although perhaps the most abstract part of his techniques, his writings on the use of the will are integral to his system. In fact, there is good reason to believe that the will is *the* key ingredient in the induction of astral projection. For despite all the stage trappings about body posture, atmospheric conditions, and so on that Lancelin outlined so diligently, there is considerable anecdotal evidence that OBEs can be induced purely through the concentrated use of willful volition. A few lucky individuals have produced OBEs by employing this method without any formal training (or even knowledge of) the Lancelin techniques.

William James, the great American psychologist and philosopher, published one such case in 1909 while he was teaching at Harvard University. The name of the projector was never revealed, but James assured his readers that he was ". . . a colleague of mine; an able and respected professor in Harvard University." The colleague had told James the story in confidence and only later wrote it in a letter. The incident had occurred in 1883 or 1884, during the time the professor was courting a lady who also lived in Cambridge.

"One evening," he wrote James, "about 9:45 o'clock, or, perhaps, nearer 10, when I had been thinking over that subject as I sat alone in my room, I resolved to try whether I could project my astral body to the presence of A. I did not at all know what the process was, but I opened my window, which looked toward A's house (though that was half a mile away and behind a hill), and sat down in a chair and *tried as hard as I could to wish myself into the presence of A* [emphasis added]. There was no light in my room. I sat there in that state of wishing for about 10 minutes. Nothing abnormal in the way of feelings happened to me."

The professor visited his fiancée the next day. She immediately told him that she had seen his apparition at 10 the previous evening while eating dinner. She had looked up from her meal to see the gentleman staring at her through the dining room door, which had been left slightly ajar. She had gone to the door to invite him in, but could find no one.

An even more elaborate set of similar attempts was recorded by S.H. Beard, a London businessman who began experimenting with astral projection in 1881. He made several visits to his fiancée, a Miss Verity, and at least one of these experiments was overseen by Edmund Gurney, a scholar who was one of the founding members of the Society for Psychical Research in England. (The Society had recently been organized to study and investigate reports of psychic phenomena.)

Beard began his experiments after reading about the nature of the will. He seemed to grasp intuitively the role that focused willing contributes to astral projection. As he wrote later, "Having been reading of the great power which the human will is capable of exercizing, I determined with the whole force of my being that I would be present in spirit in the front bedroom of the second floor of a house . . . in which slept two young ladies." These were Miss Verity (aged 25) and her eleven-year-old sister. They also lived in London.

The tests began one Sunday night in November. Beard seated himself in his room and concentrated his mind on the Verity home. The young woman knew nothing of the experiment. Beard concentrated with all his might and fell asleep with no conscious recollection of having accomplished his purpose. The following day he visited the Verity home and learned, for the first time, that he had been successful. The elder Miss

Verity told him that his apparition had suddenly appeared in her room the previous night. She had screamed in shock, awakening her sister, who also saw the apparition. Miss Verity later wrote that the incident was ". . . too vivid to be ever erased from my memory."

Beard conducted his next impromptu experiment on December 1 at 9:30 P.M.. Once again he went to his room and tried to project to a house in London where the Veritys were visiting. "I endeavored so strongly to fix my mind upon the house in which resided Miss Verity and her two sisters," he wrote in his journal, "that I seemed to be actually in the house." Beard remained there for some time. Although he could sense his physical body back in his own home, he felt paralyzed. His consciousness seemed to be across town with his fiancée. Through an effort of will, he broke the paralysis and returned to his body. Later that night, he gave himself the suggestion that he would once again appear to Miss Verity . . . this time at midnight.

Beard found that he had been successful the next day when he visited the Veritys and learned that his apparition had been seen in the hallway of the upper floor of the house at 9:30. At 12:00 Miss Verity had seen the apparition once again. She was awake in bed when the apparition suddenly appeared, entered her room, walked up to her, stroked her hair, and then disappeared.

Beard made his final attempt on March 22, 1884. Once again he focused all his concentration on the Verity home and then fell asleep. At the same time, his apparition appeared across town.

It is unfortunate that Beard conducted most of his experiments right before falling asleep and usually had no recollection of his projections. However, the critical December 1 experiment is a notable exception and confirms much of what Lancelin was discovering in France at the same general time. In this instance, Beard's act of will was so intense that he actually experienced himself at the distant location. This impression was so vivid that he genuinely felt himself *as* the apparition while remaining simultaneously aware of his paralyzed body back home. The fact that his apparition was seen by two witnesses on one occasion is strong evidence that the London businessman really was projecting some aspect of his self to the home of his fiancée.

So much for the role of conscious will. But how can unconscious will and motivation help one induce OBEs?

Earlier in this chapter, unconscious willing was defined as an all-consuming desire to attain a certain goal. This concentration must be so persistent that it becomes ever present in the mind. It could well be that this type of concentrated, yet peripheral type of concentration is also necessary for the projection of the double. In Beard's case, his desire to project to his fiancée was sparked by his study of the human will. It is likely that he had become obsessed with projecting his phantom to Miss Verity well before he actually made his first attempt. So his willful effort to project to her was only the consummation of a more general level of willing.

Sylvan Muldoon, probably America's best-known astral projector, was in full accord with Lancelin on many of these points. We know from his autobiographical *The Projection of the Astral Body*, which he wrote as a young man in the late 1920s, that he learned of Lancelin's work only after having developed the ability of conscious projection. Yet he, too, discovered that astral projection can result from an act of will. He emphasized, however, that the most important factor involved was not conscious will. The act of conscious willing acted primarily as a constant suggestion to the unconscious mind so that it, too, would will the projection. Once the desire to have OBEs becomes a matter of unconscious and pre-eminent concern, he wrote, spontaneous OBEs will then occur naturally. Muldoon called this the "passive will."

It is also possible that once one has developed the a priori ability to project, OBEs may occur spontaneously specifically through unconscious acts of will.

This happened to me in 1977 during a business trip I made to New York from my home in Los Angeles. I was awaiting publication of my first book on the out-of-body experience (my anthology, *Mind Beyond the Body*, New York, Penguin, 1978), and I was very involved in its study. I do not like to leave my home unattended, so Dave, a friend of mine, moved in to take care of it. For some reason I was worried about my house during this trip. I was concerned about my mail not being taken in, that Dave was not keeping the place locked, and a host of other worrisome little matters. I kept dwelling on them all the time.

About a week after I had left home, I began having out-of-body experiences for the first time in quite a while. After going to sleep I would suddenly find myself back in Los Angeles. I was aware that my body was in New York, and my self-awareness was very different from mere dreaming. Invariably I would find myself in the hallway of my house, and I would just look around the place for a few moments, make sure everything was in order, and then will myself back to New York. These experiences were so vivid and convincing that I told Blue Harary, who was then working in New York, about them.

The climax to this rash of OBEs came on August 22. Once again I projected to my home and decided to see if I could find Dave and make my presence known to him. I materialized in the hallway of the house, entered the spare bedroom where I had suggested Dave should sleep, but saw his brother there instead. This confused me, and I returned to my body in New York.

When I returned to Los Angeles I was greeted with quite a story! It seems that during the time I was having my experiences in New York, Dave had begun hearing odd sounds and human groans in the house. On the night of August 22—the date when I decided to make my presence known to him—Dave had seen a fleeting apparition *shooting through the hallway of the house*. This had so frightened him that he had left the house! I also learned that, just as I had seen, Dave's brother had spent the night at the house and had slept in the spare bedroom.

I might add that Dave and his brother told me these details *before* I told them about my projection experiences. The mutually corroborative evidence was, therefore, so strong that I eventually published a report on it.

This incident holds several lessons for us. It shows how the unconscious motivation to have an OBE, coupled with a pre-existing ability to experience the phenomenon, can lead to spontaneous astral projection. Many of Lancelin's ideas about learning to dynamize the will might well be meant to produce this state of a priori readiness. A constant desire to have OBEs, maintained in the mind at all times, seems one way to produce this level of unconscious readiness. In such cases, the OBEs may occur naturally even without the use of dynamic willing.

So, we may eventually find that the Lancelin techniques are an unjustly neglected approach. Certainly the experiences of Beard and James's colleague tentatively corroborate his discoveries. Very little is known about the nature of the human will; yet this aptitude we all share may be a key to the development of all sorts of psychic abilities.

REFERENCES

Carrington, Hereward. *Modern Psychical Phenomena.* New York: Dodd Mead, 1919.

Durville, Hector. Experimental researches concerning phantoms of the living. *Annals of Psychical Science,* 1908, 7, 335-44.

_____. New experiments with phantoms of the living. *Annals of Psychical Science,* 1908, 7, 464-70.

Gurney, E.; Myers, F.; Podmore, F. *Phantasms of the Living.* London: Trubner's, 1886.

James, William. A possible case of projection of the double. *Journal of the American Society for Psychical Research,* 1909, 2.

Lancelin, Charles. *Methodes de Dédoublement Personnel.* Paris: 1908.

Rogo, D. Scott. A haunting by a living agent. *Theta,* 1978, 6, 15-20.

chapter three
Projection Through Progressive Muscular Relaxation

In this age of stress and anxiety, the psychological and medical establishments are taking a renewed interest in the holistic benefits of physical relaxation. It has been aptly demonstrated that simple relaxation reduces muscle tension, alleviates anxiety, helps the body recover from illness, and benefits the mind and body in a host of other ways as well. No wonder that Dr. Herbert Benson of the Harvard Medical School found his 1975 book, *The Relaxation Response*, on the national best-seller list. Written in plain language, it extolled the virtues of relaxation and offered uncomplicated formulas by which anyone could learn the art. One subject that Dr. Benson did not touch on was astral projection; yet over the years many people have induced both spontaneous and willful OBEs by the use of relaxation techniques. Although these methods vary from authority to authority, they all stress that an OBE will take place only when the body can be stilled and quieted.

BACKGROUND

The use of some sort of relaxation exercise to induce the OBE is probably a very old art. The technique makes practical sense. We are literally the prisoners of our bodies. We are constantly bombarded by all sorts of sensory stimuli that register through the body's perceptual organs, as well as by proprioceptive stimuli—sensations that arise from within the body itself. Most of us would find it incomprehensible to think of ourselves as something apart from our bodies, which is probably one reason why OBEs are not even more common than they are. We are so chained to the body and the pleasures and sensations we receive from it that we constantly inhibit ourselves from experiencing release from its confines.

Any technique that helps us to abandon our dependence on the body may well "allow" an OBE to take place.

Dr. John Palmer of John F. Kennedy University has written that "the notion that muscular relaxation may facilitate the OBE ... makes theoretical sense because the relative lack of proprioceptive feedback from relaxed muscles may facilitate loss of body consciousness." As shown in Chapter 1, Palmer successfully used relaxation (in part) to help his volunteer college students achieve OBEs, or something akin to them. The message in all this is that one might not have to force the consciousness to leave the body in order to have an OBE, as Lancelin taught. One might merely allow an OBE to take place by working directly with the body more passively. Instead of usurping consciousness from the body, perhaps there might be a way to lower the body's guard so that consciousness can escape from it momentarily!

In this respect, it is more than revealing that many talented out-of-body travelers have quite independently induced OBEs through the use of relaxation, even though they have not been formally trained in the art of deep relaxation. Sylvan Muldoon, for instance, learned that he could induce OBEs by deliberately stilling the body and reducing his pulse rate. The primary result of this procedure was that he entered into a state of deep relaxation. (Muldoon's techniques are discussed in more depth later in this chapter.) Similar case histories could be cited as well. Blue Harary (discussed in Chapter 2), for instance, regularly employs relaxation procedures as he prepares to leave the body.

With increased interest in the art of relaxation, more and more "pop psychology" manuals are being written on just how to achieve this calm, peaceful state. It is now possible for anyone to take an hour out of the day and learn the basic techniques. With diligent practice, body relaxation can be learned within a week.

Relaxation techniques of all kinds have been around for years. The ancient yogis taught their disciples relaxation by instructing them to focus full attention on their own rhythmic breathing. Many Christian mystics also focused on breathing to quiet the mind and body as an adjunct to prayer. Another method for inducing deep relaxation was to repeat key phrases over and over along with the breathing. These methods may see much more mind-oriented than body-oriented, but remember that mind and body dynamically interact with each other. Relax one, and you automatically relax the other.

Not until fairly recently, however, were techniques for physical relaxation formally developed and taught in academic psychology. The first formally developed system was published in the 1930s when Dr. Edmund Jacobson of the University of Chicago issued his book, *Progressive Relaxation*, which explained how a state of deep relaxation could be obtained by progressively tensing and relaxing each of the body's muscle groups. Progressive self-relaxation became a popular psychological tool in the 1950s when Dr. Joseph Wolpe of the Eastern Pennsylvania State Psychiatric Institute showed that many phobias could be cured by teaching patients to remain relaxed while envisioning the object(s) of their fears.

Although Jacobson codified and formalized the practice of progressive muscular relaxation, he really did not invent it. Progressive relaxation of the body by working with the major muscle groups has been around for years. The primary virtue of Jacobson's specific exercises is that they help the subject to achieve a sense of deep relaxation, or at least appreciate the feeling of such calm. This depth is reached because the subject is constantly forced to compare the effect of relaxation to that of tension as he or she contracts and releases each muscle group.

THE TECHNIQUE

Many people relax and meditate, but not all of them end up having OBEs. Obviously, progressive muscular relaxation is only the first step to conscious control of the OBE. Inducing a state of progressive muscular relaxation (or PMR) should, therefore, be used as a state into which you must enter before actively willing an OBE to take place. Specific instructions for this combination of PMR and dynamic willing are given later in this chapter.

There are two different methods one can use to induce this form of deep relaxation. The first is to lie down comfortably and mentally go over the procedure. The other is through the use of taped instructions.

The simplest way to approach PMR is, of course, through mental exercise. There are various ways to broach the basic technique, but the following step-by-step program will accomplish the requisite task of getting you deeply relaxed.

The way you go about relaxing is, however, just as important as the exercises themselves. So, before beginning, keep the following points in mind:

1. *Find a comfortable place to begin. You can use a chair, bed, or couch, although relaxing in a prone position will probably facilitate the OBE. (One survey conducted in England some years back revealed that an overwhelming number of people who had spontaneous OBEs were lying down at the time.)*

2. *As you begin, do not tense your muscles to the point of cramping them. Just tighten them, count slowly to five, and then relax for a few seconds (10-20) before working with the next muscle group.*

3. *Focus all your attention on the feeling of tension and release. Do not allow your thoughts to wander. Keep focusing on the specific part of the body you are working with. Remember that PMR is a mental as well as a physical exercise.*

4. *Tense and release each muscle group two or three times.*

5. *While tensing each muscle group, try to keep the rest of the body still and quiet. Pretend that your whole being is located in the part of the body with which you are working.*

6. *Although this is not formally taught in many PMR programs, it might be wise to inhale as you tense, hold the breath while you count, and exhale as you release. Authorities disagree about whether your eyes should be open or closed; I would recommend keeping them closed. If you are working with your eyes open, a darkened room might be suggested.*

With the above points in mind, you can begin your specific relaxation exercises. The following is one such plan, although there are many varients:

1. *Take a series of deep breaths. Breathe in slowly, hold it for about five seconds, and then release just as slowly.*
2. *Begin by clenching your dominant fist, hold it, and count to five, release, and repeat two or three times.*
3. *Repeat the procedure by flexing the dominant bicep.*
4. *Repeat with the nondominant fist.*
5. *Repeat with the nondominant bicep.*
6. *Take a short break and concentrate on the feeling of relaxation and inner warmth, or the satisfaction that the feeling of relief gives you.*
7. *Repeat with the muscles of the forehead by either raising or furrowing your eyebrows.*
8. *Repeat by closing and opening your eyes, if you are working with your eyes open.*
9. *Repeat by clenching your jaw.*
10. *Take a short break as described in 6.*
11. *Tense and release the neck muscles by either working with the muscles or, if you have a hard time feeling this group, by touching your chin to your chest.*
12. *Tense and relax the shoulder blades by arching them backward.*
13. *Repeat by pushing your shoulders forward.*
14. *Tighten and then relax the stomach.*
15. *Repeat with the sphincter (rectal) muscle.*
16. *Repeat with the thighs.*
17. *Tense and relax the toes by curling them as tightly as you can.*
18. *Repeat by pulling your toes toward your body.*
19. *Tense and relax your dominant leg muscle.*
20. *Repeat with the nondominant leg muscle.*
21. *Stop and try not to move. Focus your mind on your state of total relaxation and enjoy it.*

Unfortunately, very few manuals explain how to return to a normal state of mind and body after going through this technique. One idea might be to begin stretching your arms and legs a few times while lying down. Stretch several of your other muscles as well, similar to the way you probably prepare to get out of bed after a long night's sleep.

The above exercises represent only a blueprint for relaxing. You may find that various alternative procedures work better for you. One variation is to begin with the feet and work progressively up the body. It probably does not matter what method of PMR you use. The important thing is to be sure you work with *all* the body's muscle groups, work at a steady and almost rhythmic rate, breathe along with the procedures, and constantly concentrate on the difference between the state of muscle tension and muscle relaxation. By the end of a week's self-training, you should be able to lose all awareness of your body after completing the exercises. This is the optimal state for undergoing OBEs, since the body will probably not automatically resist the release.

If you find it difficult to follow this type of program, you might make a tape to verbally guide you through the exercises. For best results, it helps if a female voice is used for men and a male voice for women. The speaker should use a steady, almost monotonous tone, as though reading a hypnotic induction procedure. The voice should be soft and soothing. A steady and neutral noise in the background will facilitate the effect. The sound of ocean waves striking against the shore is ideal.

The following is the text of one such relaxation tape, commonly used by parapsychologists to help people achieve an inwardly focused and ESP-conducive state of mind and body:

The purpose of this tape is to induce a state of physical and mental relaxation. We will begin with muscular relaxation. Relaxation is the elimination of all muscular tension. Get as comfortable as you can; loosen any clothing that may be too tight. When you relax, do not think about the instructions. Just follow them passively and automatically. When tensing any part of your body, remember to leave all other muscles completely relaxed. Begin by curling your toes downward into a tense position. Tense up more and more and notice the discomfort. Hold this tension while I count from 10 to 1, letting go at the count of 1. (Count) Relax. Now relax your toes completely, and feel the difference. Instead of curling your toes, arch them up toward your face and feel the tension and discomfort all along your shins. Hold this . . . (Count from 10 to 1) . . . relax. Feel the relief in your legs. Next, curl your toes again and tense up your entire legs and calves, making sure the rest of your body is completely relaxed . . . (Count) . . . relax. Enjoy the feeling of relief that accompanies the removal of muscular tension. Relax all tension, release all pressures, place your body in a state of deep relaxation, going deeper and deeper every time. Next, tense your stomach muscles as tightly as you can as I count . . . (Count) . . . relax. Let go completely. Relax. Arch your back now, and feel the tension all along your spine . . . (Count) . . . relax. Settle down comfortably again. Let go of all of your weight; let go of all of the tension in every muscle of your body. Now focus your attention on your arms and fists. Relax the rest of your body completely. Tense your fists and bend your arms at your elbows, flexing your biceps. Hold this as tightly as you can . . . (Count) . . . relax. Let your arms flop to your sides. Relax completely. Now, take in a deep breath, fill your lungs, feel the tension all over your chest. Hold it . . . exhale. Feel the relief as you exhale. Relax. Make sure that all of the body parts that we have concentrated on are completely relaxed. If there is any tension, relax those muscles completely. Now, press your head back as far as it will go. Feel the tension in the muscles of your neck . . . (Count) . . . relax. Bend your head forward now . . . touch your chest with your chin . . . (Count) . . . relax. Relax completely. Tightly squinch up all the muscles of your face and around your eyes, making a face. Hold this . . . (Count) . . . relax. Remove all strain and tension. Relax your neck . . . your throat . . . mouth . . . relax your scalp . . . smooth out the muscles of your forehead . . . relax your eyes, and all of your facial muscles. Relax . . . relax . . . relax. Relax every muscle of your body. Focus on that area which is most relaxed and imagine that same pleasant, positive, relaxing feeling to spread, engulfing your entire body in one comfortable, warm, pleasant feeling of relaxation. Relax totally and completely.

We will now begin mental relaxation. Hold your head straight and lift your eyes upward in order to strain the eyes. Do not blink. Your eyelids will become heavy; your eyelids will become tired. While waiting for this effect, take a deep breath, and while exhaling, imagine yourself becoming more deeply relaxed. Imaine relaxing more and more with each breath. When your eyes feel heavy and tired, do not force them to remain open. Close your eyes when they become tired. Take deep breaths, and with each exhalation, become more deeply relaxed. Now, concentrate again on relaxing . . . relaxing your whole body. Relax all tension . . . release all pressures. Place your body in a state of deep relaxation, going deeper and deeper. Make certain that all muscles are completely relaxed. It feels so good to be completely and totally relaxed. Noises and sounds will not distract you, but will help you to become more mentally at ease and more relaxed.

Of course, mere relaxation is not going to propel you out of the body automatically. Special procedures must be used to facilitate the OBE. Self-suggestion is the best bet, but only after you have already become adept at entering into a deep state of PMR. Here is how to combine PMR with specific OBE suggestions:

1. *As you lie down and prepare to relax, give yourself the mental suggestion that you will have an OBE at the completion of the exercises. Before beginning them, wait several seconds to allow the suggestion to register in the unconscious mind.*
2. *As you relax each muscle group and exhale, will that your mind or mental body release at that specific point. (This is a technique that Charles Lancelin recommended to induce out-of-body travel.)*
3. *At the end of the session, focus your concentration on the forehead or top of the head. Imagine your mind leaving the body by traveling right through and out of it.*

Don't expect results the first time you try this. Remember that relaxation is a skill, something you will have to learn. Since it will take practice, perhaps two or three weeks of daily discipline will be necessary before you really begin to feel how relaxation affects the body. Most authorities on relaxation do not recommend that these procedures be used at night before you go to bed, since sleep may take over before you finish. You should follow this advice at first. After you have mastered the PMR technique, however, you might try them as you lie down for your night's rest. Carry them out right in bed. When you are done, remain still on your back and let yourself fall asleep—but try to remain conscious up to the very moment that sleep overtakes you. Constantly hold in mind the suggestion that you will leave the body naturally as soon as your conscious mind slips into sleep. This technique is especially recommended by Sylvan Muldoon, who used it as one of his chief methods for inducing nocturnal OBEs.

How will you know when you are beginning to have OBEs, or are at least on the right track? Your first clue will be when you experience odd sinking and/or floating sensations as you remain relaxed. A few people suddenly find themselves just spontaneously out-of-body, but most go through a stage where they actually feel the release of consciousness. In my own case, for instance, I *always* feel as though I am sinking right through my bed or couch when I begin to have an OBE. At the same time my head begins buzzing wildly—almost as though I were standing in the middle of a busy pinball arcade.

Many people who have had spontaneous OBEs while simply resting have remarked on these same symptoms. When you begin to feel these sensations—and they can be dramatic—try to intensify them. Do not move under any condition. This will disrupt the OBE, and by this time you will probably be cataleptic anyway. Will yourself to leave the body. You might get a fright at first when these symptoms manifest, especially if you find yourself unable to move. This type of pre-OBE catalepsy is actually a good sign. Don't fight against it. If it seems that you just can't get out of body but find yourself still paralyzed, don't be too concerned. To break the catalepsy, merely focus all your attention on one of your fingers and then try to move it. The finger will invariably move, and this minor breach will overcome the catalepsy.

COMMENTS

There is considerable evidence that physical relaxation in itself is conducive to the spontaneous occurrence of the OBE. When Celia Green of the Institute of Psychophysical Research in Oxford began surveying the general public about the OBE in the 1960s, several of her informants reported that their OBEs occurred when they were meditating, relaxing, or during actual PMR exercises.

For example, one correspondent told Green how her OBEs occurred as a result of yogic meditation linked with PMR exercises. Her technique was to still each part of the body without the use of specific tension or relaxation procedures.

"I had to lie down on the floor," she wrote, "in a fairly warm atmosphere, not cold, and concentrate on putting my whole body to sleep, breathe deeply, two or three times, and let my body completely go.

"And start on my little toe of my right foot and when it was asleep, the next toe, and so on . . . on up my body, and finally my eyes, commanding my body to go to sleep . . .

"I tried this out several times of course, without too much success, and then I finally achieved it."

On one occasion the woman felt that she was drifting away. She opened her eyes and discovered that she was looking down on herself and the floor from a point somewhere above her body.

Another correspondent explained that invariably she would doze off during her relaxation exercises and an OBE could occur naturally.

". . . I always dozed off," she went on to say. "And an odd thing would happen, a sensation of being in spirit floating in the far righthand corner of my bedroom near the ceiling (always in the same position)."

The woman also discovered—as I did—that sinking and floating sensations are the first stages of a full-blown OBE. When they occurred, she knew she was about to leave the body.

Another one of Green's correspondents automatically had an OBE from sleep as a result of her relaxation exercises.

> Each night in bed, lying on my back, I relaxed my body piece by piece, starting from the toes until, finally reaching the eyes, one was supposed to concentrate on an imaginary void between the eyebrows, then, filling it with a flower image, allow this to develop into full flower.

> For weeks I simply fell asleep at waist level, as it were, and gradually the idea of leaving the physical body became neglected, although the ritual of relaxing had become a habit . . .

> Then one night in the drowsy state before sleep I was aware of a small sensation which might be likened to a tablet of soap slipping from one's grasp in the bath. I was awake . . . I turned to look at my husband and was vaguely surprised to find that I was looking down on him and as I looked I rose higher and saw my sleeping form next to his.

These cases cannot be considered anomalous. When Green asked her informants about their state of mind and body at the time of their OBEs, 33 percent of them stated that they were more relaxed than usual. Only 11 percent described themselves as more tense. This trend in the data was more substantial when Green surveyed those correspondents who had undergone more than one OBE. A little over 41 percent described themselves as more physically relaxed than normal, while 11 percent were apparently more tense.

As mentioned earlier, it is remarkable how many gifted OBE travelers have spontaneously developed relaxation techniques as a direct route to the OBE. Hugh Callaway mentioned a variant of the PMR procedure as a means he used to leave the body; and S. Keith Harary and Sylvan Muldoon have also employed some sort of relaxation technique.

Harary, for instance, maintains that his OBEs occur quite naturally as a result of quieting down the body. In a description of his technique, which he wrote especially for this book, he says:

Prior to experiencing an "at will" OBE, I induce an initial "cooling down" of my physical body. This is simply my allowing a feeling of relaxed numbness to spread through the physical body so that it will be out of my immediate conscious awareness.

During my early attempts at an "at will" OBE, I would reach this state of relaxed numbness by suggesting to myself that each part of my body would, in turn, begin to feel very heavy, warm, and relaxed. I would usually work from my feet up to my head in this way, allowing all outside thoughts to passively drift through my mind. During this "cooling down" phase, I would also suggest to myself that, if I wished, I could have an OBE and that the slightest disturbance of the physical body would immediately terminate the experience. When this was done, I was able to have an OBE.

After much practice I found that it became more and more simple for my body to enter the "cooled down" state. Eventually all I would need to do would be to suggest to myself that I would relax, that I would be able to have an OBE, and that there would be no difficulty of any sort (as there could not be difficulty unless I allowed it to occur or unless I was in an unpleasant state psychologically). A few moments after the suggestion has been given, I usually achieve the "cooled down" state "automatically." I need only concentrate on where it is I wish to "go" in the OBE, and I will go there.

Sylvan Muldoon employed a somewhat different system, although his basic principles are similar to Jacobson's PMR, since their goal is to quiet down and focus attention on each segment of the body.

Muldoon gives a full description of this technique in *The Projection of the Astral Body*. The method is not so much a specific OBE-induction technique as it is a way of placing the body in an OBE-conducive state of relaxation. Instead of working with the body's muscle groups, however, Muldoon's technique focuses on the gradual slowing of the pulse rate. Muldoon viewed this procedure as a substitute for relaxation exercises, even though specific tension-release exercises are subsumed within it. He points out that "the exercise for slowing the pulse also causes concentration and relaxation—thus eliminating the necessity of special exercises for each of these factors."

The following point-by-point program is a codification of the Muldoon relaxation method, drawn from his extensive writings:

1. *Begin by lying on your back or on the right side with your hands at your sides. (Note here the consistency with the Lancelin techniques, which also forbid lying on the left side.)*

2. *Take a deep breath, hold it for a moment, and then try to "force" the breath into the pit of the stomach. The diaphragm should expand. Then release the breath. (Again, note the similarity to the Lancelin method, which also emphasizes the role the stomach plays during the induction of an OBE.)*

3. *Repeat this procedure six to eight times.*

4. *Close your eyes and concentrate on the top of your head and try to tense the scalp muscles and then relax them.*

5. *Repeat with the neck muscles.*

6. *Repeat with the upper arms.*

7. *Repeat this process down through the entire body. At this point, of course, the Muldoon method is virtually identical to many PMR procedures, even though they were published some nine years before Edmund Jacobson—the credited founder of the PMR technique—issued his description of the method.*

8. *Focus all attention on the heart and feel its rhythmic pulsations. Concentrate on them until you can both hear and feel them without*

any difficulty. Feel them arising from within the body, but not with your hands, which should still be at your sides.

This completes the first phase of the Muldoon heart control method. You should not venture on to the next phase until you have mastered the ability to focus attention on the heart while totally relaxed. When you have reached this degree of mastery, proceed to the next step.

9. *While still lying down, try to transfer awareness of your heartbeat to any part of the body. Focus all your attention on various parts of the body and feel your heart beating there. Don't imagine it beating; you must literally* feel *the pulsations at that spot.*

10. *Beginning at your forehead, go progressively down through your body and feel your heart beating in each location—first at the scalp, then the cheeks, neck, stomach, lower abdomen, thighs, calves, and the feet.*

11. *Now reverse the procedure and go back up the body until you reach the medulla oblongata, the deep and lowest part of the brain.*

12. *Focus attention on the heart and will it to beat slower.*

The key to the OBE, according to Muldoon, is to get the heart beating slowly and steadily. In other words, you are trying to imitate the state in which the body rests during normal sleep while consciously you remain awake. This state is the natural one in which the OBE occurs.

These procedures are really not at all difficult. Modern studies in biofeedback training—the art of regulating the body's supposedly automatic functions—has proved that, with a minimum amount of practice, most people can slow or speed the heartbeat at will.

When I was toying with the Muldoon technique as a teenager, I had no difficulty mastering this ability and could lower my pulse to 60 beats per minute and then raise it to 90 within seconds. Once when I was in college, I even sadistically tormented a doctor who was trying to take my pulse by employing what I had learned! (Remember that all this was long before biofeedback became popular.) The basic problem is learning to control the heartbeat so that it remains steady. Muldoon gave some specific suggestions for learning this level of control:

We are now supposing that you are lying upon your back, re-laxed, with your arms at your sides, and that you have ac-quired the ability to feel your heart's pulsations in any part of your body. Now you are concentrating upon your heart again, and if it is not steady you are to tell it, in your mind, that it is steady, and you are to catch the rhythm of the proper beat, and beat time in your mind, concentrating upon the thump of the heart at the proper rhythm. Keep this exercise up until your heart is beating steadily.

Now, if it had before been unsteady, and you have steadied it, or if it be naturally steady and healthy, you are now ready to concentrate upon a slower beat. Think only of these pulsations. Concentrate upon these pulsations, which you feel in your chest, in your heart, beat time to them in your mind, even allowing your head to move slightly at each beat, if it be in-clined to. After keeping up this true rhythm for several minutes, begin beating time—in your mind—just a little more slowly.

Do not stop concentrating in order to determine whether or not the heart is obeying your suggestion, for you will be able to know this fact in your mind. Continue your concentration, in this manner, until you have the heart beating at the speed at which you wish it to beat.

Muldoon did not indicate just how slowly one should get the heart beating, but he mentions that, in his own case, he would lower it to 42. He did not state whether this rate was optimum for everyone.

Since at this point the body is mimicking sleep, Muldoon believed that an OBE would occur naturally. This is what he found in his own case; but then he was a natural projector. You might wish to supplement this technique with specific self-suggestions for OBE release. After you have lowered your heart rate and stilled the body, mentally command yourself to leave the body. The same type of suggestion outlined in the previous section on the PMR/OBE induction technique might best be employed.

REFERENCES

Benson, Herbert. *The Relaxation Response.* New York: Morrow, 1975.

Braud, William and Braud, Lendell. Preliminary exploration of psi-conducive states: Progressive muscular relaxation. *Journal of the American Society for Psychical Research,* 1973, *67,* 26-46.

Green, Celia. *Out-of-Body Experiences.* Oxford, England: Institute of Psychophysical Research, 1968.

Hales, Dianne. *The Complete Book of Sleep.* Reading, Mass: Addison-Wesley, 1980.

Harary, S. Keith. Personal communications to the author (January 1982).

Jacobson, Edmund. *Progressive Relaxation.* Chicago: University of Chicago Press, 1938.

Muldoon, Sylvan, and Carrington, Hereward. *The Projection of the Astral Body.* London: Rider, 1929.

chapter four
Projection Through Dietary Control

Most systems for inducing out-of-body experiences stress such mental processes as willing, visualization, concentration, focusing, and other innate skills that vary from individual to individual. The major problem with these techniques is that they are impossible to objectify. They therefore cannot be standardized. Just how much *willing* does one have to engage in to leave the body? And how can anything as abstract as the human will be quantified anyway? These are the types of questions the above techniques prompt us to ask, though they are inherently unanswerable.

Few occultists, astral projectors, or writers have ever addressed such issues, which is why the art of astral projection has remained just that—an art. There is one system that *is* objective, however, since its key is simple diet control. This method teaches that in order to undergo OBEs, one must modify the structure of the ecsomatic body through dietary regulation. Once the double's constitution and relationship to the physical body has been restructured, OBEs may occur naturally.

BACKGROUND

This method, or dietary system, is actually one phase in a complicated system that dates back to 1916. It has been completely forgotten by most authorities and writers on the out-of-body experience. Yet the story behind the publication of the system represents an important chapter in the history of psychical research.

The methods were originally published by Prescott Hall, an amateur psychic investigator from Brookline, Massachusetts, and a member of the American Society for Psychical Research. Hall was initially quite skeptical when it came to psychic phenomena, but was nonetheless intrigued by the claims of two acquaintances who maintained that they could leave the body at will. Both gentlemen also claimed that they had used their abilities of astral projection to contact new dimensions of time and space and make contact with disembodied spiritual intelligences.

Hall did not know what to think of these stories, but he remained open-minded about them . . . enough, at least, to consult a medium on the subject. In 1902, Hall had investigated an amateur medium in Boston, who had brought through some extremely evidential communications from his own deceased friends and relatives. Minnie Keeler was a homemaker, mother, and nonprofessional psychic who had developed her gifts after her husband's death. We know relatively little about her except that Prof. James Hyslop, the president of the A.S.P.R. and a critical student of the field, knew her well and had known her since the initial development of her gifts. He thought highly of her. Keeler, like most mediums of her day, would enter a light trance in order to bring through messages from the dead. Voluminous "spirit teachings" from these communicators were also delivered. By its very nature, little of the latter material was evidential, but Hyslop was impressed by the scope, literacy, and spontaneity of the communications.

Prescott Hall resumed his experiments with Minnie Keeler in 1909, and a deceased friend of his, whose identity he unfortunately kept confidential, began communicating. (In his reports, Hall refers to her only as Miss X.) His conversations with Miss X through the dissociated Keeler often focused on the subject of astral projection, and this gave him the idea for a curious experiment. If Keeler's communicators could supply him with methods for inducing OBEs *not to be found in published occult writings*, there might be an easy way to test out their credibility. If the methods worked, then obviously this information was somehow supernormally communicated through the medium. If not, the teachings were probably produced by her own unconscious mind.

During one of the sittings, Hall broached this plan to Miss X. She was intrigued with the idea and put Hall in touch with several *soi-disant* Oriental masters, who began communicating through Minnie Keeler regularly. Included among their voluminous messages were several comments and suggestions for inducing OBEs, as well as lectures on the nature of the astral body and the spiritual life. These communications were delivered to Hall at weekly intervals from 1909 to 1915. A year later, he published two lengthy but very disorganized summaries of the teachings in the *Journal* of the American Society for Psychical Research. Hyslop added a commentary in which he pointed out that, although nonevidential, he could not see how the teachings could have been a product of Mrs. Keeler's own mind.

This may seem an odd stand to take, but one must remember that the mediums of yesteryear were quite different from those of today. Many of them were totally nonprofessional. They did not give public demonstrations, accept fees, or proffer their services to strangers. Usually they discovered their gifts accidentally at table-tilting seances or other social gatherings, and viewed them more with amusement than anything else. These private mediums were often completely uninterested in either psychic phenomena or in their own gifts, and many times remained aloof from the spiritualist communities in their home towns. Sittings were usually given only to close friends and relatives.

Hyslop even made a special inquiry into Minnie Keeler's background and was satisfied that she had never formally studied psychic phenomena or psychical research. Her reading on the subject was limited to a few books, and she had casually read a periodical or two. Although Hyslop entertained the possibility that Keeler's "spirit teachings" emanated from some recess of her own subconscious mind, he felt that such a view was just as untestable as the idea that they really came from the other side of death.

Whatever one chooses to think about Minnie Keeler and her communications to Hall, they certainly represent one of the most curious chapters in the often bizarre history of the paranormal. They include very detailed lectures on the nature of astral projection, which were certainly more advanced than anything published in the popular occult literature of the day. Several techniques for inducing OBEs were outlined in these communications to which, years later, Hereward Carrington and Sylvan Muldoon would refer with utmost respect.

THE TECHNIQUES

As mentioned earlier, the Keeler system is not well organized, nor was it ever presented in a formal plan. But by reading through all of Hall's published writings on the communications, one finds that a detailed system for inducing OBEs was delivered piecemeal during the course of the Keeler sittings. The first attempt to codify these suggestions was made by Dr. Robert Crookall in 1964, but even his presentation is very unsystematic and unsatisfactory.

The Keeler system is roughly composed of three concordant aspects. The first is a diet plan that the student must follow in order to achieve the ability to have OBEs. This phase is crucial to the success of the entire system, although it has usually been downplayed by those few writers aware of this material. The second part of the system consists of several specific visualization exercises that the student should employ after he or she has been on the diet. The third part concerns certain breathing exercises to be executed at the same time as the visualization techniques. No one aspect of the system was given special emphasis. Let us look at each one in turn.

Summarizing from Hall's writings, the diet can be constructed as follows:

1. *The student should begin by either fasting or by cutting down food intake.*
2. *No food of any sort should be eaten just before an OBE attempt. Overeating may bar any success at OBE travel.*
3. *No meat should be eaten during the training program.*
4. *The diet should consist mainly of fruits and vegetables.*
5. *Carrots are extremely beneficial.*
6. *Raw eggs are favorable to the diet and to OB release.*
7. *No nuts of any kind are to be eaten.*
8. *Peanuts are especially bad.**
9. *Liquids of all types are beneficial, but are not to be used in excess.*

*I have placed peanuts in a separate category since they are not actually nuts, but belong to the pea family.

At face value, there does not seem to be anything surprising in this diet. It is generally balanced, and one young doctor to whom I showed it (without commenting on what it was meant for) noted how close it was to the famous Scarsdale Diet. His only question was why poultry wasn't included! The diet is not exclusive, either. According to Minnie Keeler's communicators, it need be followed only during the student's initial training period. After he or she has learned or acquired the ability to leave the body, the diet may be disregarded. There is, however, a correlary to the diet. During the time of experiments, the student is to abstain completely from all alcohol, tobacco, or drugs.

After maintaining this diet for some time (no duration is specified), the experimenter may proceed with conscious attempts at astral projection. These tests should be carried out while the student sits erect or in a position where blood circulation is not restricted. The feet and hands should be left uncrossed at all times. The sessions should be conducted in a darkened room and the eyes should remain closed.

After becoming comfortable, the student should begin the active OBE induction. Leaving the body can be facilitated by absorption in any of the following visualization strategies:

1. *Imagine yourself inside a cone and passing through it. Try to pop out through the top of the cone after squeezing yourself in.*

2. *Concentrate on the image of a whirlpool. Imagine yourself swirling through the vortex and out the body. You should imagine yourself becoming a single point and then expanding as you emerge.*

3. *Imagine yourself being carried along on a wave.*

4. *Imagine yourself clinging to a coil of rope and being drawn out of the body by it.*

5. *Imagine yourself whirling about—and then whirl yourself right out of the body. Or imagine yourself being drawn out through a revolving tube.*

6. *Imagine that you are in a tube gradually filling with water. See yourself as a point of light and try to find a tiny hole in the side of the tube from which to escape. Push yourself through it.*

7. *Build up an image of yourself as though you were looking at yourself in a mirror. Then transfer your consciousness to that image.*

8.   *Imagine steam rising from a limp cloth; then imagine that you are*
     that steam emerging from (the cloth of) your physical body.

These initial visualization exercises are rather varied, yet a few of them are peculiarly fascinating and may well work for inducing OBEs. For instance, take the image of being pulled up through the body by a rope. While experimenting with astral projection as a teenager, I once underwent a very bizarre experience during which I felt that I was literally being pulled out of my body and through the head by a rope. The unmistakable sensation was very strange and a bit unsettling, since it seemed I was leaving the body against my will. So, concentrating on such an image might feasibly prompt this experience.

Other visualization techniques recommended by Keeler's communicators seem to relate to sensations that people proficient with the OBE have actually reported. A few stress the role of whirling and spiraling out of the body. There are many reports on record from people who have actually experienced themselves revolving or whirling right out of the body, and usually through the head. The mirror-image technique is also similar to Sylvan Muldoon's suggestion that one stare into a mirror and practice shifting consciousness from one image to the other. In this case, however, it is likely that Muldoon was borrowing from Hall's writings without proper credit.

The idea of visualizing yourself popping through some sort of opening has also been suggested by some psychics quite independently of Keeler. Hugh Callaway often left his body by imagining himself exiting his body through a trapdoor at the top of his head. Aleister Crowley, the famous British occultist, taught his students to leave their bodies by imagining a closed door on an otherwise blank wall inscribed with a symbol the student has used for meditation. The student then induces an OBE by imagining the door opening and him- or herself passing through it.

Two years after publishing these methods, Hall issued his last report on the Keeler communications, which contained the results of his own experiments with them. Several more visualization exercises were outlined at that time, including:

1.   *Concentrate on a space a yard or two in front of the body and try to*
     move forward to it.
2.   *Concentrate on a spot above your head and try to rise up to it.*

3. Concentrate on a point one foot and several inches above your head and try to merge with it.

4. Sit erect in a chair, but do not lean against its back. Concentrate on a horizontal bar just above your line of sight. Focus on the bar until you feel yourself rising, and then hold your breath.

5. Lie down, brace your hands and feet, and contract your stomach muscles while trying to force the astral body out; or imagine yourself—your physical body—falling through space.

6. Imagine yourself walking up a flight of stairs. At the top of the flight take hold of an imaginary rope and jump off. Fill your lungs with air at the same time.

7. Sit in a chair and try to feel yourself moving forward horizontally.

8. Imagine yourself whirling about on tiptoe and then springing or taking off.

9. Imagine yourself as a soap bubble floating in space.

10. Imagine yourself flying to the Himalayas through the air.

11. Imagine a point two feet in front of your throat. Then imagine it moving toward you until you merge with it.

All these additional exercises may seem redundant and unsystematic, like their predecessors, yet they all share several things in common. They are excellent techniques for concentration, since they are very simple images that can be held in the mind's eye without much difficulty. They also teach the student to focus concentration away from the body. As mentioned in the previous chapter, we may be chained to the body because we are habitually being reminded of its presence. These reminders come through sensory stimulation and proprioceptive stimuli. The exercises listed above are all useful for stilling the body so that its access to sensory stimuli is reduced. Focusing the mind away from the body could well help the individual ignore, if not exactly reduce, proprioceptive stimulation normally arising from within the body.

If interpreted in this light, the Keeler communications make considerable sense.

The third part of the Keeler/Hall methods relate to breathing, a practice that has always been of utmost interest to occultists, yogis, and other purveyors of the spiritual path. Unfortunately, this aspect of the method is not spelled out very well in Hall's published writings. We learn only that Keeler's communicators taught that "breathing is important as the pulse in the brain is synchronous with it." They added that "various exercises" will help one leave the body and that "for getting out of the body, *holding the breath* is of value, but holding it out has no effect."

Keeler's communicators never elaborated on just what these "various breathing exercises" consisted of. Their remarks on breathing are cryptic at best and may seem rather hopeless. Could it be that a key element of the Keeler method has been lost to us?

I do not think so. Enough information is given in the messages for us to reassemble what techniques the communicators were referring to. It seems probable that the brief comments quoted above refer to a very ancient breathing technique taught in yoga (called *pranayama*), which reportedly leads to the development of psychic gifts, including the ability to leave the body at will. This technique consists of inhaling at a steady rate, holding the breath a prescribed period of time, and then exhaling. These three phases must follow a consistent ratio of intake, hold, and exhalation, and they must be repeated several times. Since this technique is described in detail in the next chapter, it will not be outlined here. But the way Keeler's communicators emphasize the intake and retention of breath is too coincidental with the philosophy of Yogic pranayama to be happenstance.

It is also interesting that most Yogic writings stress that these breathing exercises can be dangerous if not practiced correctly. The dangers, they warn, may be both spiritual and physical. Could this be the reason that Mrs. Keeler's communicators were reticent about describing them in detail?

To sum up: the Keeler/Hall system encompasses three aspects. One must begin by following a prescribed diet for an unstated period. For the actual induction of the OBE, one must sit or lie down with hands and feet uncrossed and mentally carry out various visualization exercises. Breathing exercises should be conducted at the same time. This system is much like progressive muscular relaxation in that it is a passive system, unlike the Lancelin method, which might be called an active system. It teaches one how to quietly relax the body, not fight your way out!

COMMENTS

Just how valid are the Keeler/Hall methods?

There are two ways by which the Keeler material and methods can be analyzed. The first is to determine whether the communications contain information about the OBE that Minnie Keeler herself could not normally have known. The second is through the records of anyone who has tried to induce the OBE by following these techniques.

It was the late Robert Crookall, the Bath, England, geologist and parapsychologist, who first showed how evidential the Keeler material seems to be. In 1964 he published a short volume in which he demonstrated that many facts about astral projection, so diligently outlined in the communications, were not commonly known at the turn of the century. Remember that these techniques were delivered from 1909 to 1915, a period when hardly anything was known about the OBE. While Hugh Callaway had already begun writing about his experiences, Forhan's work was virtually unknown in the United States, and Muldoon had not yet popularized the subject. Not even very many psychical researchers had taken much interest in the phenomenon. Keeler, had she actually wanted to learn about the OBE, would have had few sources upon which to draw.

Our knowledge about the experiential and phenomenological aspects of the OBE came about only in the 1960s. In the late 1950s, Crookall retired from his geological career to study the OBE on a full-time basis. His first project was to amass several hundred case reports and then carefully and statistically map out their characteristics. His first work appeared in 1961 and a supplementary analysis of even more cases were published in 1964. These two reports, each published in book form, were the first studies ever to analyze the precise patterns and phenomenology of the experience. About this time, too, Celia Green in Oxford began her own systematic study of OBE narratives. So today we are in a perfect position to evaluate the Keeler material.

It certainly looks as though her communicators knew much more about the OBE than anyone alive at the time. For instance, on one occasion, Keeler's Oriental masters told Hall that OBEs sometimes occurred as a result of undergoing anesthesia. They warned, however, that such OBEs are less vivid and more unfocused than OBEs that occur more natually.

This seems to be true. We now know that many people undergo OBEs during the administration of ether, nitrous oxide, or sodium pentathol. Both Crookall and Green collected many such reports in their work. Crookall found 46 such cases in his initial collection of 382 accounts, which, therefore, constitute 12 percent of his sample. But when he took a closer look at these cases, he made an even more interesting discovery. For the purpose of analysis, Crookall broke down his case collection into two general categories. The first consisted of OBEs that had occurred naturally and spontaneously—as a result of sleep onset, when the person was ill or exhausted. In the other category, he placed OBEs enforced through suffocation, hypnosis, or through the use of anesthetics. Between these two types of OBEs, he found a qualitative difference. "Natural" OBEs were much more vivid, mind-expanding, and peaceful than the enforced ones, which tended to be dull and unfocused. Although the differences Crookall found between natural and enforced projections were not generally statistically significant, owing to the small sample of enforced cases he had to work with, they do represent an obvious trend that would indicate a genuine experiential difference between the two types of cases.

Keeler's communicators also noted that during the onset of the experience, a momentary blackout takes place at the moment the consciousness shifts its locus from within the physical body to the ecsomatic body. "At the moment of separation of the two bodies," Hall was told, "there is usually a moment of unconsciousness."

Crookall found that this phenomenon is quite common to his cases, and his analysis demonstrates that 20 to 30 percent of all people who report OBEs will experience this effect.

Hall was told that, at the onset of the OBE, the subject will go through a phase of dual consciousness, that is, a phase when he or she will be able to experience him- or herself both in and out of the body at the same time. Even if still in the body at these times, he or she may even be able to sense or see spirit presences, such as those of the dead, nearby.

This has also turned out to be true. Sylvan Muldoon wrote extensively on the subject of dual consciousness. It also crops up often in the writings of people who have only had one or two such experiences. For example, one of the most famous of all OBE cases ever reported was placed on record by Sir (later Lord) Auckland Geddes in an address he gave to the Royal Medical Society of Edinburgh in 1937. Geddes, a celebrated physician and professor of anatomy, originally reported that the experience had been related to him by a friend, but most writers on the subject agree that he was describing a personal experience.

Geddes reported that one night he awoke deathly sick. He was so weak that he could not get to the phone; he could only lay back and wait for death to overtake him. Suddenly he felt his consciousness dividing itself into two parts. One part remained with his physical body; the other seemed to be above his body as a blue cloud. He was aware of himself in bed, yet at the same time he could look down on himself from his out-of-body position. Finally, he felt all his vitality pass from the body on the bed into the blue cloud. He—or the cloud—then detached itself from the body and moved about the house. While traveling in this state, Geddes saw his wife enter his room, discover him, and call the local doctor. He watched in disdain as the doctor arrived and gave him an injection to revitalize him. As his heart began to beat again, he found himself being sucked back into his body. He described himself as "intensely annoyed" by having to return!

Although Dr. Geddes did not perceive any spirit presences while out-of-body, many people do—just as Keeler's communicators said. Crookall includes some 62 such reports in his case studies. It is well known that people who have OBEs as the result of heart failure or life-threatening accidents often experience leaving the body, traveling to a world of beauty, and meeting deceased relatives who instruct them to return to their bodies. It is *not* as well known that individuals who have had spontaneous OBEs sometimes report similar encounters. Often they sense rather than see these entities, who either accompany them on their out-of-body voyages or urge them to return. This is perhaps one of the most interesting, although neglected, aspects of the OBE.

The Oriental masters who so readily shared their wisdom with Hall also explained something about the actual mechanisms of astral projection. The chief means of leaving the body is through the head, they maintained, and sometimes the projector will experience him- or herself spinning out of the body.

Hall had no way of knowing that Crookall would verify this fact many years later. His case studies include 29 incidents in which the reporters specifically described leaving the body through the head. These were physical sensations, too, and not just images. Having experienced this phenomenon myself, I can vouch for how stunning the effect can be. It often feels as if your inner self were being sucked out right through a hole in the top of your head! It is, no doubt, for this reason that Hugh Callaway suggested leaving the body by focusing attention toward that point.

Spiraling out of the body is a rare experience, yet Muldoon described this phenomenon in his autobiographical writings and other cases could be cited as well.

Keeler's communicators also described the (now) well-known "silver cord," which so many people see connecting their physical and ecsomatic bodies, how persons undergoing an OBE may see streaks of light behind them as they travel,* how a person may find him- or herself floating horizontally above his or her body after first leaving the body, and a host of other little known features that we now know to be part and parcel of the OBE syndrome. It is, therefore, hard to disagree with Crookall when he writes that "It is now clear that Mrs. Keeler's communicators, whoever or whatever they were, knew a great deal more about astral projection [than] any other living person." Crookall also maintained that this fact alone indicates that the teachings most likely came from discarnate intelligences.

I personally believe this last issue is moot. It is also possible that they emanated from some higher aspect of Minnie Keeler's own mind—a level of mind much more wise about us and our metaphysical nature than we are consciously aware.**

It matters very little whether Keeler's communications were delivered by the dead or by her own inner self. The main point is that the information contains a wealth of data about the OBE, of which Mrs. Keeler could hardly have been aware. That the teachings are certainly more sophisticated than any material available at the time is circumstan-

---

*Forhan (writing as Yram) specifically notes this phenomenon on pages 62 and 66 of his Practical Astral Projection; see also page 13 of Sylvan Muldoon's Projection of the Astral Body.

**There is a great deal of psychological literature on this aspect of the self, which more and more physicians, psychologists, and psychiatrists are being forced to confront. This level of mind can be tapped through hypnosis and has been formally called "the hidden observer." It is a part of ourselves that just sits back in our minds and observes and evaluates whatever happens to us. People suffering from multiple personality often exhibit at least one personality that is much saner, wiser, or more benign than all the rest. This personality, which has been called the Inner Self-Helper, can even help a clinician cure the victim! A doctor I know in Los Angeles has found that he can contact this aspect of the mind, which he calls the Protector Self, to help him diagnose refractory patients. All of these researchers seem to be describing the same aspect of the mind. This level of mind could probably also communicate to us and to others by taking on its own individuality. Some mediumistic guides may be of this sort. The ever-popular Seth, who communicates regularly through Jane Roberts of Elmira, New York, may be just such a persona.

tial evidence that the induction techniques are also both valid and important.

Now we come to a more practical evaluation of the Keeler methods. Have they ever worked for anyone?

Prescott Hall experimented with these exercises for several years, beginning with their initial inception in 1909. He apparently experimented from his home in Brookline, Massachusetts, and kept detailed diaries of his results. Apart from the material on astral projection, Hall also received considerable information on psychic development in general. Most of these were meditation and visualization procedures. He eventually became more interested in developing clairvoyance and clairaudience than the ability to leave the body. This was probably because Keeler's communicators advised him at the onset of his sittings that his ecsomatic vehicle was very strongly attached to his physical body and that he would have a difficult time learning to project. His experiments with astral projection were, therefore, not systematic, although he did toy with the Keeler suggestions on and off over a six-year period.

Hall apparently had his first partial success in September 1909. He reports in his diary that, while visualizing, he felt that his physical body was "falling down and away." He also noted a definite feeling that he was not in the body at all. Hall does not mention just how long the sensation lasted. During some experiments he conducted in October, he had similar success. He felt as though he were being drawn out of his body during his exercises and thought he was actually being pulled out of his body by an unseen force. His diary entries for March 1910 reveal that he was beginning to experience odd sinking sensations during his experiments.

Unfortunately, Hall apparently never succeeded in having a full-blown OBE. He did have some peripheral or incipient OBEs, but was never able to get over the "hump" and experience true conscious out-of-body travel.

This all makes considerable sense to me. During those periods when I start having OBEs, I go through a phase in which I have similar falling and sinking sensations when I retire at night. This is the first indication that an OBE or an OBE period is beginning to manifest. When I first feel these sensations, I have to focus all my will on leaving the body. A great struggle usually ensues, and I battle against my body's pull. Sometimes I manage to escape. Many times, however, I lose control of the sensation and find myself securely stuck back inside. Hall probably underwent a similar problem.

There is even some evidence in the Keeler communications to this effect. Hall told Mrs. Keeler's communicators of his success at a sitting held in 1909. They in turn suggested that when these feelings manifested, he should tense his stomach, brace his hands and feet, and try to force his way out of the body. They also told him to visualize himself floating in space at the same time. It is interesting that this is the *only* place in the entire Keeler communications where the Oriental masters suggested a dynamic and active approach to OBE induction. They must have been aware that Hall was coming close to leaving the body and were willing to offer special exercises for him to follow. When I reach this state, I intuitively hold my breath, close my eyes, and imagine myself leaving the body and floating above it. I chanced upon this technique long before I read about Hall's experiences.

His failure to leave the body successfully might have been predicted, however. In Hall's 1918 report to the American Society for Psychical Research, he specifically notes that he did not follow the communicators' recommendations about abstaining from tobacco and alcohol. It might even be surmised that Hall probably did not follow the dietary plan either, and since this dietary plan is a critical part of the Keeler material, it can hardly be maintained that Hall's experiments represent a critical test of the techniques.

One other experimenter has also tested the Keeler methods. His results were much different and actually led to the development of out-of-body talents. As you might have guessed from this buildup, that researcher is myself!

I first learned about the Keeler/Hall material during the spring of 1965. I was a teenager and had recently decided that parapsychology was going to be my life's work. I was not too interested in developing psychic ability myself, chiefly because I did not believe I possessed any. I was more concerned with conducting investigations, working with people who really were psychic, and running experiments. But when I started reading about the out-of-body experience, I knew that I just had to experience it. I soon devoured everything I could find on the subject, hoping to find some information on how to induce the experience. Muldoon's *The Projection of the Astral Body* became a virtual bible to me, since he outlined several of his own techniques in the book.

That summer, my desire to undergo an OBE became particularly intense. After classes were over for the day, I would invariably come home, go to my room, and practice the teachings I had read about. I also experimented nightly. During this period many memories came back to me of a series of OBEs I had undergone as a young child. At night, when I was about four or five years old, I would wake from sleep, float above my bed, travel down the hall of my house, and then return to my room. I also began recalling that some sort of guide, whom I sensed rather than saw, often accompanied me on these trips—as though he was trying to teach me something.

These memories were not confabulations either. I specifically remembered just which playmates and family members I shared my secret with. Today, these memories are just as vivid and clear as my memories of high school and college.

These recollections only fueled my interest in the OBE since they demonstrated that I had at least the potential for out-of-body travel. It was while looking for a sure way to undergo out-of-body travel that I found a summary of the Prescott Hall material in Carrington's introduction to Muldoon's first book.

I did not know anything about Minnie Keeler or her Oriental masters, since Muldoon and Carrington mention practically nothing about this aspect of Hall's writings. My interest was chiefly centered on the dietary regulations he outlined. They were easy to follow, did not demand much time, and did not get boring! I did revise them, however. I kept on eating meat, but limited my intake and avoided meat that was cooked rare. (I had read somewhere that this was the thing to do if you could not avoid eating meat.) I ate my eggs cooked, not raw, but gorged myself on carrots and avoided nuts like the plague—even to the point of obnoxiously picking them out of bakery products.

The weeks came and went. By August I still had not achieved success with my attempts at astral projection, so I gave up trying. I kept on with the diet plan since it was convenient to do so, but I relinquished any other experimentation. Naturally, I had no conscious expectation of having an OBE from then on.

Then it happened.

It was a blistering hot day in August. I came home as usual in the early afternoon after summer school classes, turned on the radio in my room, and threw myself on my bed. As I listened to an aria from Wagner's

Rienzi, I began to doze off. I was in that twilight zone between waking and sleeping when suddenly it felt as if my whole body were sinking right through the mattress. I had never felt anything like it before. I was startled, but merely turned over onto my left side. Then it dawned on me that I might be having an OBE. The sinking sensations continued, so I turned onto my back.

Instantly I found myself paralyzed. I closed my eyes and concentrated all my attention on intensifying the sensations. My face felt numb. I must have blacked out for a moment, for the next I knew, I felt myself floating above my body and then found myself standing next to the foot of my bed, looking at myself. My vision was fairly clear, but it appeared as though everything in the room was enveloped by a light mist or fog. After looking at myself for a while and wondering just what I should do, I decided to attempt to get out of my bedroom. I floated around almost instantaneously and for the first time noted that I seemed to be an apparitional duplicate of myself. I moved toward the door without actually walking, but my equilibrium was off and I fell to the side. Instantly I became upright again and continued moving toward the closed door. I unfortunately blacked out then and awoke back in my body. My heartbeat seemed abnormally slow.

The entire affair must only have lasted a minute or so, for the same aria was still playing. I was elated by the experience, but despite the vividness of the OBE, I did not resume any conscious experimentations to induce it. I did not have to—for only a few weeks later, it all happened again.

Again I returned from school, went to my room, and lay down on my back to take a nap. I felt the same weird falling sensations that had heralded my first OBE, but this time they were accompanied by pulsations as though my whole body were being charged with electricity. As I had done previously, I began to concentrate on intensifying the sensations. Once again I experienced a momentary blackout and found myself out-of-body, this time crouching next to the bed toward some cabinets. My vision was a bit blurred and something seemed to be obstructing my left eye. I stood up and looked at my body in hopes of seeing the famous "silver cord" I had read so much about. I did not see it, but did note that my (physical) head had fallen to the side and onto my left shoulder. My arm was pushing up against my left eye. That, I surmised, was why my vision in the apparitional body was likewise obstructed.

More than anything else, I wanted to get out of the bedroom. So I moved toward my bedroom door and tried to pass right through it. It worked. One moment I was in my room, approaching the door; the next thing I knew I was emerging from the door on the other side. I traveled around the corner of the hallway and into the living room where I saw my mother on the couch reading. At that moment my two dogs began barking and I blacked out. An instant later, I "awoke" back in the body.

These two experiences were the only ones I had that summer. I still did not continue experimenting with conscious projection and even went off the Keeler diet plan. I really did not expect any more OBEs, and my mind was now more attuned to beginning the new school year.

Then in October, much to my surprise, I began having other OBEs. One night after I had gone to bed, I was drifting off to sleep when I suddenly found myself totally paralyzed. Horrendous gushing sounds filled my ears as though there were a waterfall right outside my window. At the same time I felt I was being pulled out of my body through my head. The sensation was very unpleasant, so I tried to abort the experience. I broke the catalepsy by concentrating on moving my index finger, and then rolled over onto my left side, which is supposed to preclude leaving the body. As I began to shift position, however, three grotesque white faces suddenly appeared, hovering in the air. They seemed positively menacing, and even after they vanished, I was terrified. If this was astral projection, I wanted no more of it!

A few weeks later the same thing happened. I had awakened from sleep with the feeling that I had been on a long journey to an unknown place, but before I could even get my bearings, I felt as though I were literally being catapulted from my physical body. Odd as this may seem, I suddenly experienced myself as a disembodied point in space in the corner of my room. . . and looked down at *both* my physical body and my ecsomatic form that was hovering above it. The sensation of floating was not as intimidating as before, and I just let myself flow with it. This state lasted a few moments, and then my consciousness slowly extinguished and I found myself back in the body. The experience was quite puzzling to me, and only years later did I read about other cases of "dual release" projection.

This particular OBE served as a springboard for my abilities, and I underwent dozens of nocturnal OBEs over the next two years. I even learned how to partially control them. But this is a story that I will leave for the chapter on dream control methods, since this technique was intricately related to the state of initial sleep onset.

What role did the Keeler dietary plan play in the development of my OB skills? This is a complicated issue, and I am far from sure that I can offer a definitive answer. Many systems for inducing OBEs stress the role that unconscious motivation plays in learning to leave the body. It could be that while I had given up my conscious attempts at projection, I was still *unconsciously* willing them to occur. By withdrawing my conscious attention from this task, I may have strengthened this other level of willing. If this was the case, the Keeler methods had very little to do with the onset of my OBEs.

Several factors, however, lead me to believe that the Keeler diet may have contributed to my ability to leave the body.

When I first stumbled onto the Hall material, I knew nothing about his tie-in with Minnie Keeler, her Oriental communicators, or Prescott Hall's own experiences. When I went off the diet, I naturally expected my OBEs to end. They did not, and this puzzled me so much that I began to doubt that the diet had materially contributed to the experiences in the first place. Only two years later did I read the Keeler material in the original form and learned that, according to the communicators, *one can expect OBEs to continue even after the diet has been dispensed with.* If my OBEs were produced through unconscious psychological suggestion, they should not have continued the way they did. Also, the records Hall kept on his own attempts at astral projection describe the same incipient phases of the OBE that I encountered while following the Keeler method. Even when reading Hall's autobiographical notes today, I am astounded by the similarities between his observations and my own.

The Keeler methods also emphasize the role that imagery and visualization play as an adjunct to the diet. I had never been aware of my mental imagery before my first OBEs. But as I had more and more of them, my powers of visualization became extremely active. I started having very vivid hypnagogic images (images that precede sleep), although I had never been aware of them before. Could it be that the Keeler diet somehow affects one's powers of mental imagery and visualization? Could the exercises the communicators offered be based on actual hypnagogic images that begin to manifest as one follows the diet?

This is all pure speculation, of course. But I have long felt that the Keeler material *was* somehow integral to my sudden development of out-

of-body skills. And when dealing with anything as mysterious as leaving
the body, sometimes intuition is the best thing to go on.

REFERENCES

Alvarado, Carlos. Phenomenological differences between natural and en-
forced out-of-body experiences: a re-analysis of Crookall's findings.
Theta, 1981, *9*, 19-11.
Crookall, Robert. *The Techniques of Astral Projection*. London: Aquarian
Press, 1964.
_____. *More Astral Projections*. London: Aquarian Press, 1964.
Forhan, Marcel Louis (Yram). *Practical Astral Projection*. London: Rider,
n.d.
Hall, Prescott. Digest of spirit teachings received through Mrs. Minnie E.
Keeler. *Journal of the American Society for Psychical Research*,
1916, *10*, 632-60, 679-708.
_____. Experiments in astral projection. *Journal of the American Society
for Psychical Research*, 1918, *12*, 39-60.
Muldoon, Sylvan, and Carrington, Hereward. *The Projection of the Astral
Body*. London: Rider, 1929.
Rogo, D. Scott. Experiential aspects of out-of-body experiences. In *Mind
Beyond the Body*, D. Scott Rogo, ed. New York: Penguin Books,
1978.

chapter five
Projection Through Breathing, Yoga, and Mantra

The phenomenon of astral projection is known to just about every culture in the world. Although it seems to be a relatively common experience, many cultures revere the OBE as holy, numinous, or transcendental. The shamans and holy men of many primitive societies prove their powers by exercising this ability, which ranks with levitation and fire-immunity as evidence of their great powers. It is perhaps for this reason that the spiritual disciplines of many religions lay forth methods for developing out-of-body talents.

These methods vary and are structured according to the belief systems of each world-view. Many of these techniques have been lost to us. For centuries, ancient Greeks seeking the path of enlightenment traveled to the temple at Eleusis, where they were spiritually reborn after participating in several days of sacred rites. There is some indication that part of these rites consisted of undergoing an OBE. But if so, the actual techniques used for this ritual induction have been lost to posterity.

Although the priests of Eleusis guarded their secrets well, vast oral traditions about leaving the body *have* come down to us from India and Tibet. Not only does yoga prescribe systems for leaving the body, but Tibetan Buddhism—which was greatly influenced by the occult tradition of Indian cosmology—contains elaborate doctrines about astral projection, the astral body, and the feats it can perform. Some of these doctrines are similar to traditional Taoist teachings and even to Cabalism, the secret mystical teachings of Judaism.

BACKGROUND

The practice of traditional yoga is so ancient that no one knows when and how it first evolved. It may well have been practiced in India as long ago as 3,000 B.C. Yoga is not really one religious system, but a series of interconnected disciplines, all of which purportedly lead the practitioner to mystic union with God. The practice of yoga today consists chiefly of detailed instructions and exercises for breathing, body control, meditation, and devotion. These procedures were first systematized by Patanjali, an Indian scholar and practitioner of the art, in his famous *Yoga Sutras*, which date back to the second and third centuries B.C. Patanjali did not invent these practices, but merely codified them from the spiritual practices of his day.

There really does not appear to be anything too esoteric about the basic teachings of yoga. The *Yoga Sutras* themselves are fairly straightforward and comment very little on psychic phenomena or how the ability to produce such wonders may be developed. Later yogic teachings, however, do emphasize this aspect of the discipline—an aspect no doubt contained in a vast, secret, and oral tradition that Patanjali shied from commenting on. The OBE is particularly described in the *Hatha Yoga Pradipika*, which surfaced during the twelfth century. Alain Danielou, one of France's greatest experts on Indian religion and lore, quoted over a half-dozen additional Hindu texts on the astral body in his *Yoga—the method of re-intergration*. Astral projection is specifically listed as one of the "30 subsidiary attainments" achievable through yoga. The more occult side of yoga also teaches specific exercises for projecting the subtle body.

As noted above, there are various systems of yoga, including the yoga of mastering control of the body *(hatha* yoga), the yoga of awakening dormant energies in the body *(Kundalini* yoga), the yoga of sound and chanting *(mantra* yoga), the yoga of devotional acts *(bhakti* yoga), the yoga of good deeds *(karma* yoga), and yogas of mind-stilling and meditation *(gnana* and *raja* yoga). The most important of these for our purposes are those that relate to the control of superphysical energies within the body. Kundalini yoga and mantra yoga, which is sometimes and partially subsumed within it, teach that a dormant energy rests within all of us. Lying at the base of the spine, the Kundalini, when awakened, travels up the body by coiling up the spine. It awakens several "psychic centers," or *chakras*, as it rises toward the head. Each chakra is linked to specific psychic gifts, which develop spontaneously as the center is stimulated. It is not clear whether these centers are merely figurative focal points of the body or are actual objective centers of psychic power. Many authorities hold differing opinions, but most agree that the awakening of these centers is the key to the acquisition of supernormal power—which includes everything from levitation, to astral projection, to control of other people's actions, to creating matter through the power of thought.

There seems little doubt that the deeper traditions of yoga deliberately map out methods for attaining psychic powers. Specific exercises for mastering some of these are outlined in the teachings quite openly.

Westerners point out that true yoga actually warns the student against focusing on the development of psychic gifts, considering them distractions on the path to spiritual enlightenment. However, the issue is just not that simple. The great *Yoga Sutras* of Patanjali do warn that certain psychic abilities may be detrimental to the spiritual quest, but this warning does not pertain to such phenomena as levitation, astral projection, and so on, which are continually promised to the student as just rewards for commitment. Later yogic writings, such as the *Hatha Yoga Pradipika*, virtually promise the development of psychic gifts (or *siddhis)* as a result of diligent study and practice. Some of the older *Upanishads* of Hinduism also warn the student about psychic abilities; but while advising against openly displaying them, nothing detrimental is said about developing them.

There are several steps to the mastery of yoga, including the development of right thinking, mastery of body postures, correct breathing, and profound contemplation. Psychic phenomena and their development are especially related to the art of correct breathing, or *pranayama*, which is linked to the raising of the Kundalini. Hindu philosophy teaches that the universe is pervaded by a subtle energy called *prana*. To proceed on the spiritual path, one must be able to manipulate this energy and imbue the body with it. A whole system of yoga has been built on various techniques for correct breathing, each prescribed as a specific way of manipulating prana. Hereward Carrington, an authority on yoga as well as on psychic phenomena, once wrote that breathing is "the most important keystone of the whole Yoga system." Since breathing ignites the Kundalini, breathing becomes the single most important route to ecstasy—including the power to leave the body at will.

Mantra yoga is related to the idea that there are rhythms to the universe into which one must enter to achieve transcendence. Mantra yoga teaches that certain sounds have special powers when chanted over and over. Although some writers on yoga argue that the traditional mantras are only focusing aids, the true traditions teach that the very sounds of the words or phrases can materially influence the world.

The paranormal traditions of yoga were especially cultivated in Tibet. The primitive ways of the Himalayan people were largely animistic and obsessively concerned with the supernatural. Even today the supernatural plays a large role in their world-view and rituals. When yoga and (later) Buddhist philosophy were introduced, Tibet developed its own homegrown religion, which incorporated Buddhist cosmology, yogic practices, and primitive superstition. Tantric Buddhism resulted, which teaches highly elaborate and ritualistic doctrines and practices about psychic phenomena. The holy writings of Tibet, the *Bkah-Hgyur* and the *Bstan-Hgyur*, are loaded with references to astral projection, and specific methods for achieving the ability are included within their yogic traditions.

Very similar beliefs and doctrines have arisen quite independently in other cultures. Taoism, one of the indigenous religions of China, teaches not only about the traditional Kundalini of yoga, but also important methods of breathing. Cabalism, the mystical system of meditation developed within the Hebrew tradition, also stresses the dynamic role of the breath in meditation. It even teaches a symbolic cosmology similar to the chakra system, and has its own version of traditional mantra yoga. Reciting the names of the Hebrew characters or certain transmutations of the letters that form God's sacred name are employed. The great Cabalists also taught secret breathing techniques. Doctrines about the soul's ability to leave the body appear in the *Zohar*, an important Cabalistic text that surfaced in Spain in the Middle Ages.

Neither is Christianity exempt. Several of the great Catholic mystics achieved ecstasy through meditation accompanied by rhythmic breathing and the continual repetition of certain prayers. Roman Catholic traditions mention bilocation, the phenomenon of appearing in two places at the same time. Many of the great mystics and saints of the Church were (and are) adept at it. Unlike most Eastern philosophies, however, the mystical theology of Catholicism does not contain any specific techniques for leaving the body, since all supernormal gifts are interpreted as gifts from God.

An entire book could be written on the role that the subtle body and astral projection plays within the cosmology of most mystical traditions. But let us turn our attention to those techniques used to induce the out-of-body experience.

THE TECHNIQUES

The yogic term for the astral body is the *linga sharira.* Its projection is called *prapti,* or the art of instantaneous travel. One method for inducing the OBE is through breathing. At least two specific exercises exist for leaving the body, but the student should familiarize him- or herself with the basics of correct breathing techniques before going on to these more advanced practices.

Most Westerners simply do not breathe correctly. Correct breathing stems from the diaphram, not from the chest. This method of breathing must be learned before the student can go on to any further practices. The following steps show you how to breathe correctly.

1. *Assume an erect position, standing or sitting. Lying down flat with your hands at your sides (called in yoga the "corpse posture") may also be used. Some students prefer to assume a formal lotus or half-lotus position (with the feet tucked into the lap).*
2. *Breathe slowly and steadily through the nostrils. Let your abdomen extend. Do not breathe from the chest.*
3. *As you breathe in through the diaphram, gradually swell the lower chest, thus pushing out the lower ribs.*
4. *Continue to fill yourself with air and begin to extend the upper chest, thus pushing out the lower ribs.*
5. *Hold the breath for a few moments.*
6. *Exhale slowly, forcing all the air out of the lungs. Exhale through the nostrils or through a combination of the nostrils and mouth.*

There is nothing mystical about this exercise. Although originally outlined in yoga, this form of breathing is regularly taught to instrumentalists, singers, and athletes for breath control.

After learning this basic technique, proceed by perfecting a few other basic yogic exercises. One is called "the rising breath," which can be used to vitalize the entire body.

1. *Stand up straight with your heels together.*
2. *Inhale steadily. At the same time, raise up on your toes as the air fills your lungs.*
3. *Hold the breath and your stance for several seconds.*
4. *Exhale slowly through the nostrils at the same rate you inhaled. Lower yourself accordingly.*
5. *You may want to raise and lower your arms at the same time you breathe in and out.*

The "prolonged" breath is also a basic and simple yogic exercise that will prepare you for the deeper mysteries of pranayama. Remember that these exercises have a hidden as well as a practical side, since they spread prana throughout the body.

1. *Stand or sit erect.*
2. *Draw in the breath slowly and steadily.*
3. *Hold the breath as long as you can without discomfort.*
4. *Exhale by forcing the air out of your body through the mouth in short gusts.*

These preliminary exercises will prepare you for the actual system of pranayama developed for the practice of out-of-body travel. The first part of the practice is called the "great psychic breath." It was first outlined by Yogi Ramacharaka, the pen name of an Englishman who studied yoga and became a keen student of it around the turn of the century. His writings, which appeared as a series of short handbooks, are excellent guides to the study of yoga. The idea behind the great psychic breath is to prepare the system for the development of psychic abilities by initially stimulating the chakra system. As Ramacharaka explains in his *Hindu-Yogi Science of Breath*, the exercise reduces to 11 steps.

1. *Lie in a relaxed position.*
2. *Breath steadily and rhythmically until the rhythm is perfectly established.*
3. *As you inhale and exhale, imagine the breath being drawn up the body through the bones of the legs and then forced out of them.*
4. *Repeat, but focus on the bones of the arms.*
5. *Repeat, but focus on the skull.*
6. *Repeat through the stomach.*
7. *Repeat through the genitals.*
8. *Imagine the breath being drawn up the spinal column and then back down as you exhale.*
9. *Imagine the breath being inhaled and exhaled through every pore of the skin. Envision the entire body being filled with prana.*
10. *Send the breath, with every subsequent intake of air, to each of the body's vital centers: forehead, back of the head, base of the brain, solar plexus, lower part of the spine, navel, genitals.*
11. *Exhale all the breath from the lungs, stop a moment, and then squeeze every bit of residual air out of the body.*

Ramacharaka also mentions that this technique, coupled with meditation, can lead to the projection of the subtle body. The basic technique is to meditate on the inner self as something apart from the physical body and independent of it. This procedure will train your mind to ignore the body during meditation, which may allow the release of the etheric double. Breathing must be kept rhythmic at all times during the contemplation.

Having completed this practice, the student is now ready for the quintessential out-of-body exercise—the practice of cross-breathing, an ancient yogic secret passed on from guru to disciple. It was kept secret because of its great power not only to induce the OBE, but to awaken the Kundalini and even cause levitation to occur. The art was hardly known at all in the West until Swami Vivekananda, a disciple of the famous guru Ramakrishna, visited the United States in the 1880s and, much to the horror of his fellow yogis, popularized some of the more esoteric practices of yoga.

The basic system is relatively simple, although its precise execution can be tricky:

1. *Plug your left nostril with your left thumb and breathe through your right nostril.*

2. *Continue inhaling until your lungs are filled to capacity, but not to the point where you feel uncomfortable.*

3. *Plug your right nostril with your right thumb and begin counting from one to 100 until you can no longer hold your breath comfortably. Of course, keep the left nostril plugged at the same time.*

4. *Remove your left thumb and exhale slowly through your left nostril, without straining or forcing the breath.*

5. *Begin inhaling again, this time through your left nostril while the right nostril is plugged.*

6. *Hold your breath again and begin counting.*

7. *When you have reached the same number as before, remove your right thumb and exhale through your right nostril.*

The key to this system is moderation. If you inhale too much air the first time around, you may have to gasp for breath at the end of the cycle. If this happens, you are exercising incorrectly. Never hold your breath longer on subsequent cycles than you did during your first trial. This can upset the carbon dioxide level in your blood. The object of the exercise is to hold the breath longer and longer, but this must be done *gradually* and over an extended period of time.

A special relationship must also exist between the time you take to inhale, hold, and exhale the breath. There should be a strict ratio between the phases. You should begin by using 12 seconds for inhaling, 48 seconds for holding the breath, and 24 seconds for exhaling. Your goal is to increase this ratio to 16:64:32 and, finally, to 20:80:40. However, some scholars prescribe different time factors, although they all prescribe the 1:4:2 ratio. One well-known text published at the turn of the century suggests beginning with 4:16:8, increasing to 8:32:16, and finishing with 16:64:32.

Each ratio system corresponds to a different level of pranayama, with the development of psychic abilities related to the third phase of the exercise.

For maximum effect, most ancient scriptures recommend 20 cycles of cross-breathing for each session. Just how often you should perform the exercise is not stipulated, but four times a day would not be unreasonable.

You might schedule sessions when you wake up, before lunch, before dinner, and when you are preparing to retire. Remember to practice on an empty stomach.

Some manuals suggest that you mentally recite a mantra while cross-breathing, but this does not seem to be necessary. However, repeating one of these "words of power" may help you keep track of how many seconds go by in each phase of the exercise. The basic sound *AUM* is usually recommended.

As mentioned before, various authorities on yoga recommend cross-breathing for different purposes. Some scholars, such as Sir John Woodruffe (who wrote under the name Arthur Avalon), suggest cross-breathing as a means for levitating. Woodruffe was an Englishman who wrote some of the first scholarly treatises on Eastern religion just after the turn of the century. Even today, practitioners of Transcendental Meditation teach the exercise to advanced students seeking to develop this siddhi. Despite their claims, however, there is no evidence that any practitioner of TM has actually levitated as a result of it. Swami Vivekananda, on the other hand, recommended cross-breathing for awakening the Kundalini. He makes only one revision to the exercise. The student is instructed to send the breath-current down to the base of the spine mentally while holding it. Yet other practicing yogis suggest the use of this technique as a means for projecting the etheric body. Perhaps cross-breathing leads to all of these great gifts.

Whatever the case, yogic scripture also tells the student how to know when he or she is on the right track. The body will begin to perspire; it will feel light as though ready to float away; and the student may hear curious internal sounds—such as musical tones, chimes, flutterings, and other "seed" sounds—when the ability to leave the body is being enhanced. These sounds are purportedly produced by the *nadis,* or energy carriers, in the body as they begin to activate.*

It is not clear whether cross-breathing is supposed to actually induce the OBE on the spot, or even help the student prepare him- or herself for spontaneous projections. But there are suggestions in the literature that

---

*Prescott Hall often heard such sounds during his experiments with the Keeler methods. See also a curious report in the December 1919 <u>Proceedings</u> of the American Society for Psychical Research, which concerns a man who accidentally began leaving his body as a result of practicing automatic writing. A description of many of these precise seed sounds are given, although the man had never studied yoga.

cross-breathing is a method for the *deliberate* and *applied* projection of the subtle body.

Another system for leaving the body was developed in Tibet some time later. This technique is highly systemized and so elaborate that it would take an entire chapter just to outline it. It includes four prayers to be (apparently) recited as one conducts a few preliminary visualization exercises focusing on various Tibetan deities. This is to be followed by about 15 or 20 further visualization exercises, which sometimes require the student to hold more than one image in the mind at the same time. Certain mantras are to be chanted at various points in these visualizations. There are also different visualizations prescribed for different feats that the yogi wishes to accomplish through the OBE. And this is only the written part of the formula! Supposedly, "secret" adjuncts exist for these visualizations that remain within the oral tradition of Tibetan yoga and that have never been placed in print.

For those readers who wish to attempt astral projection through this elaborate method, it is outlined on pages 261-73 of the Standard Oxford University Press edition of W.Y. Evan-Wentz's authoritative *Tibetan Yoga and Secret Doctrines.*

Yoga and Tantric Buddhism are not the only disciplines that teach how astral projection can result from mantra reciting. Ritual chanting is also prescribed in Cabalism, the set of doctrines and practices that constitute vast mystical traditions within Judaism.

Originally an oral tradition, the written records of the Cabalah culminated in the Middle Ages when its most esoteric tract, the *Zohar,* appeared in thirteenth century Spain. Just as in yoga, Cabalism's goal is to bring the person into direct union with God. Its practices are varied, but they prescribe methods of meditation, breathing, and the repetition of certain biblical phrases or letter combinations. The best-known meditation aid is to focus attention on certain letter combinations transmuted from those in the sacred name of God. Chanting key biblical phrases, so that one sees "beyond their meaning," is another old Cabalistic method.

A system for deliberately leaving the body through such recitation was outlined by Franz Bardon, a German Cabalist, in his *Der Schlüssed für wahren Kabbalah,* which offers several Cabalistic practices and formulas. The book is difficult to understand and the method of reciting these special letter combinations is left rather cryptic. For example, it is not clear whether the combinations are to be chanted aloud or recited mentally. In 1964, however, Cuno Helmuth Müller extracted the key ingredient of the Bardon methods and systemized them for general use. In a series of articles contributed to the German occult magazine *Die andere Welt*, Müller describes Bardon's mantra method for out-of-body travel in some detail. The practice allegedly culminates in the projection of the etheric body, the apparitional and semiphysical replica of the physical body.

The practice begins with the recitation of four letter combinations:

DC, DK, EF, EK

Each combination should be chanted seven times for one complete rhythm. After several recitations of the complete rhythm, one proceeds to the next. Each rhythm should be chanted for between 10 to 15 minutes. Therefore, it will take at least 40 minutes for each session. A sitting position should be adopted for the exercise, similar to one you might use for meditation. These letter combinations should be recited daily for two or three months before the rest of the letter combinations are added.

At that time, seven more combinations are adjoined so that the complete mantra reads:

DC, CK, EF, EK
BF, CR, DR, EB, BD, BN, CU

Once again, a complete cycle consists of seven repetitions. Each of the preliminary group should be chanted for about five minutes. The second set should be recited for 10 to 15 minutes; an entire session will last 90 minutes or so.

It is not exactly clear how the OBE is supposed to manifest. Apparently, this technique either directly induces OBEs or makes the practitioner OBE-prone so that they begin to occur spontaneously.

The major problem with this system is just how the letters are to be enunciated. The German system is based on an alleged Hebraic tradition. At least one diligent (and dedicated!) German occultist has actually employed this method successfully in his native language. (See my comments below.) Yet, to be authentic, the original mantra must have been intended to be recited in Hebrew. According to Cabalistic tradition, speaking or merely writing the letters of the Hebrew alphabet contains great power. The only problem is that there are no character names for the vowels. They are given markings but no formal names. So, in Hebrew the mantra would read:

daleph-chaf/ chaf-kaf/ (e)fay/(e)kaf
beth-fay/ chaf-rash/ daleph-rash/ (e)beth/ beth-daleph/ beth-noon/chaf (u)

The recitation of the vowels remains a puzzle.

Even the use of the character "chaf" does not really relate to the letter "c" since a gutteral "ch" sound and character designation is the only comparable translation. This is a problem we run into in German as well. Apart from personal names and adopted foreign words, the letter "c" is used only in conjunction with the "ch" or "ck" combination. So, how would it fit into even a genuine German Cabalistic tradition?

Another problem with this system is the demands it makes on memory. It might, therefore, be wise to write out the letter combinations, preferably in Hebrew, on a poster before reciting them. Such a procedure would certainly not be alien to Cabalism, since this tradition directly teaches one to meditate on the letters of the Hebrew alphabet. Even the act of writing them out is a prescribed Cabalistic practice. Any basic Hebrew primer will give you the corresponding characters related to daleph, chaf, and the rest of the alphabet, as well as the signs for the vowels. Walter K. Paul, whose experiments with this system are discussed later, has also noted that this formula may be mentally recited as well as verbalized with effect. So, perhaps it may be best merely to contemplate the letter combinations rather than recite them orally.

Although the Müller system does not include the use of any particular breathing exercises, Cabalism in general placed great emphasis on how the breath links us to all creation. We also know that the great rabbis taught secret methods of breathing as part of their students' training. These methods have been lost to us. All we do know is that secret breathing exercises were combined with visualization exercises—such as imagining the breath saturating the brain—to produce mystical union with God. In all likelihood, these practices were similar to the cross-breathing or the great psychic breath of traditional yoga. So, the use of some sort of rhythmic breathing exercise might be combined with the mantra for the best results.

COMMENTS

As with most methods for inducing OBEs, these spiritual practices rest or fall on their practical application. If they do work, there should be some record of it.

At least tentative documentation shows that the great yogis of the East are proficient in the art of out-of-body travel. Dr. Karlis Osis of the American Society for Psychical Research and Dr. Erlendur Haraldsson, a psychologist from the University of Rekjavik in Iceland, visited India in the early 1970s hoping to document the feats of the great gurus. They heard astounding stories of miraculous bilocations and were able personally to investigate two such reports.

The first concerns Satya Sai Baba, southern India's most celebrated guru and alleged wonder-worker. While attempting to document his purported miracles, the two psychologists heard that on one occasion in 1965 Sai Baba had been "seen" in the city of Manjeree in Kerala, while at the same time holding company with some of his followers at his ashram miles away. Ram Mohan Rao, director of a technical school in Manjeree, claimed that Sai Baba had suddenly appeared on his doorstep, stayed with him and his house guests for quite some time, and then departed. Osis and Haraldsson were eventually able to locate eight witnesses who had been present at Rao's home when Sai Baba appeared. They were also able to document the fact that Sai Baba was at his ashram at the same time.

The case is weakened, however, by the fact that none of the witnesses at Rao's home had ever met Sai Baba before his unexpected visit. They recognized him only through pictures they later saw; so the visitor *could* have been an imposter posing as the guru.

A more evidential report concerns Dadaji, a lesser known holy man who had originally been a prominent singer and businessman. He left society to study yoga and reappeared with his new identity and abilities after his initiation onto the spiritual path. Osis and Haraldsson were eager to investigate the guru after hearing the following story.

Early in 1970, Dadaji was visiting some devotees in Allahabad, a city 400 miles from his home, when he suddenly announced that he was going to the prayer room of the house. When he emerged some time later, he told his followers that he had astral-projected to Calcutta and claimed to have visited the home of a devotee's sister-in-law. He urged the group to contact the woman and verify his story. His followers did so and found that, at the same time he had secluded himself in their own prayer room, he had indeed been seen in Calcutta. The woman's family related how the guru had initially materialized in the room of their daughter, who was herself one of his disciples. She recognized him immediately, which shocked and surprised her no end. His sudden and initially transparent appearance caused her to scream, which alerted the rest of the family to his arrival. His figure was seen by several of the family, including the head of the household, who had been a total skeptic until he saw the mysterious figure sitting in the girl's room.

Osis and Haraldsson tracked down several witnesses to the case, including Dadaji's hosts in Allahabad and the family in Calcutta. All the evidence was mutually corroborative.

Since the gurus of India are somewhat proficient in the art of astral projection, this fact alone serves as circumstantial evidence that the traditional OBE induction methods of yoga may be legitimate. But there is even stronger evidence that pranayama techniques may be a road to astral projection, and it comes from the West, where cases of pranayama-produced OBEs have also been reported.

Attila von Szalay is a gifted psychic and yogic practitioner who has lived in southern California for many years. I first met him in 1967. Art von Szalay was born in New York, but traveled west in the 1940s to work as a photographer. His psychic abilities developed spontaneously when he was a young man, which led him to study yoga. After mastering the art, his psychic abilities blossomed, including the ability to leave the body at will. He even took particular delight in popping in on people now and then.

A chief witness to von Szalay's remarkable abilities is Raymond Bayless, a 25-year veteran of Los Angeles's psychic scene and a long-time collaborator of mine. Bayless has been able to document several examples of von Szalay's ability at astral projection, psychic photography, and telepathy. One day in February 1955, as Bayless explains in his book, *Experiences of a Psychical Researcher,* he was sitting at home on a couch tying a shoelace when he saw a flickering movement out of the corner of his eye. Thinking his cat had run across the room, he looked up to see a large trapezoidal "shadow" hovering in front of him! It was the height of a man and was floating about a foot off the ground. As he watched in astonishment, the shadow flew through the room and out an open glass door.

Bayless had no idea what the shadow signified, but he immediately drove to Hollywood to tell von Szalay what he had seen. When von Szalay answered the door to his studio, Bayless did not even wait to get inside before telling his story. "Guess what happened to me," he began. Von Szalay promptly replied, with no coaxing whatsoever, "You saw me." He then explained that he had consciously projected to his friend, and he described the interior of the Bayless's house, although he had never visited there.

Von Szalay later told me that he produced this OBE through a form of pranayama. His particular technique was to lie down and then take a series of short, shallow breaths, which were then ejected forcefully from the lungs. He would produce this hyperventilation for several minutes until he found himself out-of-body. He feels that this breathing exercise, which developed from his study of yoga, causes a minor form of oxygen starvation in the system, which automatically induces the phenomenon.

Bayless himself has toyed with various pranayama techniques for leaving the body, and he had some success on at least one occasion. One experiment he conducted in 1952 was particularly enlightening. It was late in the afternoon, and Raymond decided to try leaving the body through breathing exercises. He stretched out on his bed in the *shavasana,* or corpse position, with his arms at his sides. He then engaged in a practice akin to the great psychic breath, by rhythmically breathing in and out in a quick but deep fashion. At the same time, he mentally willed that he should leave the body and also visualized the Kundalini at the base of his spine. He practiced for about an hour before quitting. Then he just rested and let his mind wander off into daydreams. His eyes were closed.

By this time, Bayless was not expecting to leave the body. But as he rested, he felt his body begin to sway violently from side to side. His first impression was that an earthquake had struck. No sooner had he thought of this than he felt himself falling back down to the bed. The experience was so dramatic that he was shocked by its intensity and realized that he had actually been floating *above* his body in an out-of-body state. He feels, however, that it may have been his faith in the technique rather than the breathing itself that produced the incipient OBE.

The accounts of Art von Szalay and Raymond Bayless may seem a little facile, but their experiences were definitely not examples of "beginner's luck." Remember that both these men had been toying with yoga and yogic breathing for many years before their experiences occurred. This practice may have, therefore, readied their bodies for the OBE. And while

Bayless tends to eschew pranayama as a uniquely viable system for inducing the OBE, von Szalay believes that breathing may be the virtual key to the ability.

Just why breathing relates to the induction of the OBE is not clear. Yogic cosmology offers a complicated explanation based on the way breathing links the human to the pranic forces of nature. There might be simpler factors involved, too. Recent research conducted at the Langley Porter Neuro-psychiatric Institute in San Francisco has shown that deep breathing has many effects on the mind and body. It relaxes the system, calms brain activity, and induces the production of alpha waves, while at the same time relieving body tension. This state of mental and physical calmness is probably conducive to the state necessary for leaving the body.

Nonetheless, yogic cross-breathing is one OBE induction procedure that should be approached with the utmost caution. . . if at all. It is a very unfocused technique meant to raise the Kundalini, produce levitation, and develop a number of other paranormal abilities including astral projection. Ancient yogic scripture stresses that these breathing exercises should not be divorced from a more general practice of yoga and should be practiced only under the guidance of a teacher. If done incorrectly or prematurely, tradition warns that the Kundalini might be aroused in the wrong way. This could seriously disrupt the body's energy system and produce all sorts of disquieting physical and mental effects.

This is why the cross-breathing technique was kept secret until Vivekananda revealed it to the West, for which he was severely criticized by other gurus. Perhaps this is why the Cabalists also kept their breathing techniques so secret. Warnings about haphazardly experimenting with yogic breathing are conspicuously evident in yogic literature, and there is good reason to take these admonitions seriously. Many students of yoga have succeeded in raising the Kundalini through cross-breathing, but they have had all sorts of negative reactions to the experience, including unbearable and uncontrollable flashes or waves of heat over the body, attacks of panic and terror, chronic insomnia, compulsive tics, and even transient episodes of psychosis.*

*For some case histories, see Lee Sannella, M.D., Kundalini—psychosis or transendence? (San Francisco: Henry Dakin, 1976). There is also a fascinating report in the December 1919 Proceedings of the A.S.P.R. to which I referred in an earlier footnote. The report concerned a man who contacted the A.S.P.R. in 1906 about some psychic experiences he was having. He was on the verge of a total psychotic

There is no reason not to take these reports seriously. Such reactions probably represent genuine disturbances caused by the improper manipulation of an energy housed in the body and as yet unknown to conventional science. My personal belief in the cogency of these warnings stems from talks I have had with yoga students who have actually experienced extremely adverse reactions to Kundalini yoga. Since pranayama is part of an elaborate mental/physical/spiritual discipline meant primarily to rouse the Kundalini, perhaps it should not be the procedure of choice for attempting out-of-body travel. There are many other systems available, and few of these appear to possess any inherent dangers.

Nor is there too much to recommend in the Tibetan techniques. First of all, few people reading this book would probably be enthralled by a method that takes 20 pages just to explain—with parts of the technique that are still secret and must be handed down from teacher to student. Does this ritual actually work, however? This ridiculously elaborate and often nonsensical ritual may actually be a smokescreen. The yogis of Tibet must have had much simpler methods for inducing the OBE, but published this elongated ritual to dissuade the public from taking an interest in the matter. It may have been meant to discourage interest in the OBE and probably little more. This is just my own speculation, of course, but the sheer elaborateness of the system is so different from anything taught in any other discipline that I cannot help but consider it bogus.

Now let us turn to Cabalism.

Despite the unwieldiness of the Müller mantra system, it has been successfully employed by German occultists. Walter K. Paul, a German spiritualist, published a complete report on his use of the system in the spring 1968 issue of *Light*, the official publication of the College of Psychic Studies in London.

Paul began his experiments in January 1965 by using the mantra daily. His first success came six weeks later when he awoke from sleep to find himself floating over his physical body in a phantom duplicate. The experience lasted from 15 to 20 seconds, and then he experienced a

---

breakdown and kept babbling about a force at the bottom of his spine that would periodically act up. When the force rose up his body and struck his head, he would go crazy. Luckily, he had found a way to control the force through breathing. He also had begun experiencing moments when his mind would leave the body. Needless to say, the man had no knowledge of yoga and had stumbled on all of this by accident. He was eventually "cured" through hypnotic suggestion.

momentary blackout and awoke in his body. The same thing happened two months later as a result of a conscious attempt at astral projection. Upon going to bed, he "willed" himself to leave the body, but nothing happened. He awoke sometime later and immediately felt his body vibrating. He remained motionless and then experienced his etheric "leg" raise out of his physical body and then back down again.

His next experience came the next night, when he had a full-blown release. He was just about to fall asleep when the vibrations began again. This startled him back into a waking state, and as he lay motionless, he felt himself rising right out of his body. "At that moment," he writes, "I felt an arm under my back which was pulling me sideways, and I felt the bed-cover slip." His first thought was that he was actually being carried out of bed. Then he realized he was having an out-of-body experience, which was somehow being aided by a discarnate being. "He put me on my feet," continued Paul, "to the left of the bed, a little way from the foot, and behind me, with a hand on both shoulders." Paul's impression was that the friendly helper was keeping him from falling. "Then he or she turned me to the right and pushed me gently, and I walked till I stood directly in front of the foot of my bed." Paul then blacked out and came to back in his physical body.

Paul's account is virtually identical to my own childhood experiences. I, too, felt as though the presence that accompanied me on my first OBEs was virtually carrying me (that is, my etheric double) through the house. He was apparently "spotting me" the way one spots a weight-lifter. Although my recollections are dim on this specific point, I do remember seeing this helper on at least one occasion.

Paul had an identical experience two months later. He awoke to find himself standing in the hall in front of his bedroom. At first he thought he had been sleepwalking, so he went back to his room. He experienced a bizarre sucking sensation as he approached his bed as though a vacuum were being formed around his bed, and this odd sensation alerted him to his out-of-body state. The bedroom was dark, so he sat down at the foot of his bed and actually *felt* his physical body there. Within a moment he awoke *in* bed. The entire episode had lasted 30 or 40 seconds.

These OBEs lasted for several months, during which time Paul diligently continued his mantra recitations. They apparently stopped when Paul ceased the exercise.

Paul returned to his Cabalistic practices two years later, curious as to whether he could induce OBEs by mentally reviewing the formulas instead of reciting them. After six weeks of daily practice, he began having OBEs once again. They were primarily nocturnal experiences and would begin with a sense of bodily vibration. When these sensations arose, Paul would simply will himself out-of-the-body. This would cause him to float out of his body, usually coming to rest at the foot of his bed. These incidents were less prolonged and complex than his earlier OBEs, which Paul believes may have resulted from his purely mental use of the letter combinations.

These records speak for themselves. It is interesting, however, to see the curious parallel that crops up in both Paul's and Bayless's accounts, which also appears in my own records. Note that Paul's OBEs occurred spontaneously after he had gone to bed. They did not manifest as a direct result of the mantra recitation itself. Likewise, Bayless had his OBE only after he had finished his pranayama exercises and was simply lying still. My first OBEs also manifested spontaneously after I had ceased consciously trying to induce them. Despite the fact that we were using totally different induction methods, this curious "release of effort" phenomenon occurs in all three cases. This pattern may be telling us something very important about the ability to leave the body. An occult explanation would be that many of the exercises used to induce leaving the body—visualization, diet, mantra sayings, and breathing—somehow alter the structure of the etheric body or its relationship to the physical body. This alteration may then lead to the spontaneous manifestation of the OBE.

The "release of effort" may, however, be explained psychologically. The various induction techniques we have been reviewing, as well as those that have been described in previous chapters, may serve simply to focus attention on the intent of having an OBE. They dynamize the will, as Lancelin would have said, and serve as perpetual unconscious suggestions that an OBE will indeed eventually take place. Once the conscious mind has been removed from the task of willing the OBE, this release of effort allows the suggestion to work totally within the unconscious—which then orchestrates the experience.

If this is the case, the release of effort phenomenon is a very important aspect of astral projection. Its message may be simple. . . that it is our motivation to have an OBE, and not the use of any particular system, that actually grants us the ability to leave the body.

REFERENCES

Bayless, Raymond. *Experiences of a Psychical Researcher.* New Hyde Park, N.Y.: University Books, 1972.

Carrington, Hereward. *Higher Psychical Development.* New York: Dodd Mead, 1924.

Danielou, Alain. *Yoga—the method of reintegration.* London: Christopher Jones, 1949.

Epstein, Perle. *Kabbalah—the way of the Jewish mystic.* Garden City, N.Y.: Doubleday, 1978.

Evans-Wentz, W.Y. *Tibetan Yoga and Secret Doctrines.* Oxford, England: Oxford University Press, 1958.

Gibson, Walter. *The Key to Yoga.* New York: Key Books, 1958.

Ingber, Dina. Brain breathing. *Science Digest,* 1981, *89,* 72-75.

Osis, Karlis, and **Haraldsson, Erlendur.** OBEs in Indian swamis: Sathya Sai Baba and Dadaji. In *Research in Parapsychology-1975.* Metuchen, N. J.: Scarecrow Press, 1976.

Paul, Walter K. Out of the body by mantras. *Light,* 1968, *88,* 26-40.

Richards, Steve. *Levitation.* Wellingborough, England: Aquarian Press, 1980.

White, John, ed. *Kundalini, Evolution and Enlightenment.* Garden City, N.Y.: Anchor/Doubleday, 1979.

Yogi Ramacharaka. *The Hindu-Yogi Science of Breath.* Chicago: Yogi Publishing Society, 1904.

chapter six
The
Monroe Techniques

Most of the procedures discussed so far represent formal systems for the induction of the OBE, designed for widespread and general use. In this chapter we'll be looking at some highly specific techniques developed by a gifted OB traveler, which he has found useful for his own projections. Every gifted subject—from Sylvan Muldoon to S. Keith Harary—has developed a unique method for leaving the body. Luckily for us, these methods have usually been placed on record.

BACKGROUND

Probably the most popular and successful book ever written about the OBE appeared in 1971 when Robert Monroe, a Virginia businessman, published his autobiographical account, *Journeys Out of the Body*. Monroe, now a white-haired executive, was born in 1915 and grew up in Lexington, Kentucky. He graduated from Ohio State University and worked first in New York's radio and television industry. From there he moved to advertising. He began experiencing OBEs in 1958 long after he had built a successful career. At first he was confused by his new-found talent, but over the years he has become a frequent traveler along the astral by-ways. His book describes not only his terrestrial OBEs, but surrealistic journeys to parallel universes and other dimensions of time and space. As he stated in a *Fate* magazine interview, he has even had "certain remarkable experiences—such as visits to other energy systems that the 'I' consciousness could not even conceive of. There has also been contact with entitites that are far beyond anything I've ever dreamed of in my wildest fantasies."

According to his autobiography, this businessman developed his out-of-body talents as a result of an illness that struck him in the spring of 1958. His family had gone out one day, and he had spent his time listening to a tape of specially prepared sounds. After brunch with his family when they returned, he decided to lie down and was suddenly seized by cramps. His first thought was that he was suffering from food poisoning, so he stayed in bed all day and rested.

The same thing happened three weeks later, but during this attack, his whole body began vibrating. Even though these weird vibrations continued to plague him for months, his family doctor could not diagnose the problem.

One night he was lying in bed with his arm draped over the side, dangling near the rug, when the vibrations began manifesting again. Monroe pushed on the floor, and his hand seemed to pass right through it! He was puzzled but shrugged off the experience as a daydream. The vibrations continued to manifest.

His first genuine OBE occurred a few weeks later. Monroe was just about to fall asleep when he felt a wave of vibration surge through his body. His thoughts instinctively turned toward gliding, which was his current hobby, and suddenly he found himself near the ceiling of his bedroom. "I was floating against the ceiling, bouncing gently with any movement I made," he writes. "I rolled in the air, startled, and looked down. There in the dim light below me, was the bed. There were two figures lying in the bed. To the right was my wife. Beside her was someone else. Both seemed asleep." It was, of course, his own figure lying there. Monroe began to panic when he realized he might be dying, so he dove down and back into his body.

This experience so puzzled Monroe that he began consulting his doctor and a psychologist friend about his syndrome. The psychologist recommended that he read up on Eastern philosophy, but even this did not allay Monroe's fear that he was going insane. Nor did it help much when more OBEs began manifesting over the next weeks. These continued incidents eventually led him to the U.C.L.A. Neuropsychiatric Institute in 1964, where he met with several of the staff in hopes of learning more about his problem. They, of course, knew nothing about the OBE and so were hardly helpful. Luckily for him, however, he learned about parapsychology at about this same time, which gave him a clue toward understanding his experiences.

When he found out just what he was actually experiencing, Monroe lost his fear of the OBE. Instead of dreading his projections, he began experimenting with them—soon learning that he could not only leave the body, but visit his friends (even if they were miles away) and journey to parallel universes. He also began keeping detailed records of these incidents, complete with the names of the people he had visited while out-of-body, what they were doing at the time of his visitations, and on the subsequent verifications of his observations.

His strange journeys also made him prone to some curious side effects. During the preliminary phases of his OBEs, he started having precognitive visions. His curiosity about the experience also brought him into contact with the scientific establishment, and he eventually took part in research projects both at the University of Virginia and the Topeka (Kansas) Veterans Administration Hospital, where he tried to induce his OBEs under controlled conditions.

Monroe's chief concern, however, has been to develop means of leaving the body and exploring the new dimensions of reality that he has discovered through his experiences. Not only has he developed many personal techniques, but he has opened his own institute for the development of more effective procedures. The foothills of the Blue Ridge Mountains of Virginia are the current home of the Monroe Institute for Applied Sciences, which opened in the early 1970s. Clients of the Institute can spend several days there, during which they undergo a training program in self-discovery, hopefully including a classic OBE. The sessions include sensory isolation practice, auditory stimulation, and guided imagery.

The work of Robert Monroe is, therefore, dichotemized. On one hand, he is interested in the experimental and scientific study of the OBE, and on the other, he—like Hugh Callaway and Marcel Louis Forhan before him—has become fascinated with the occult side of the experience, which promises to teach us about a hidden dimension of the universe.

THE TECHNIQUES

Monroe has developed several methods for leaving the body, based primarily on his own personal experiences. He has revised these techniques considerably over the years, and the program currently taught at the Monroe Institute is very different from the methods he originally recommended in 1971 when his autobiography was published. In January 1982, a spokesperson for the Institute specifically told me that Monroe's original writings on OBE induction practices (circa 1971) are now outmoded. Such a great difference exists between his autobiographical writings and his current week-long program that some description of each should be given. In this section we will be looking at those methods that Monroe himself used to leave the body and that, according to his own account, he used when he successfully produced his OBEs in the laboratory. In the next section, we'll be taking a look at his Institute's program.

Monroe clearly believes that the OBE is a human potential we are all capable of developing. He has even written that "the only possible way for an individual to appreciate the reality of the Second Body and existence within it is to experience it for himself." He adds, noncommittally however, that "whether or not anyone *should* is beyond the scope of my judgment."

Monroe contends that before actually attempting to leave the body, various a priori conditions must be met. Chief among these is the intense desire to have an OBE, which is probably similar to what earlier writers referred to as the "will" to experience the state. He also stresses that the experimenter must possess a certain degree of psychological strength. After first leaving the body, Monroe began having chronic OBEs. Somehow he had opened a door that could no longer be shut. He advises the student that he or she must reckon with this same problem. Having once induced an OBE, there is no turning back. You will have to live with your decision to leave the body for the rest of your life.

Your next problem will be dealing with your friends and relatives. Leaving the body is an ability that places you in a new relationship with those around you. You must be willing to be labeled a freak, insane, or merely a liar, since many of your friends and relatives will not be willing to accept the validity of your experiences. You must also be prepared for a certain amount of ostracism.

Monroe's warnings are well taken, especially when so many members of the general public are becoming interested in spiritual growth. Hugh Callaway was an occultist, Sylvan Muldoon a spiritualist, and Marcel Louis Forhan a mystic who lived in China for a good portion of his life. These men moved in social circles that were totally open-minded to claims of the paranormal. You might not find yourself in the same position.

Take the case of a young hospital worker who developed rather remarkable psychokinetic abilities after months of self-development and practice. Her ability to move small objects through the power of thought was filmed, and two top American parapsychological laboratories documented her abilities. Yet, she eventually renounced her gift. She had no problem handling this talent she had unleashed within herself, but she could not handle the reactions of her friends, who were generally ignorant of parapsychology and held no belief in psychic phenomena. They believed that she was merely pulling a sham or was simply self-deluded, and they became very suspicious of her. The emotional strain caused by this ostracism was too great, and finally the young woman ceased demonstrating her ability altogether. Today she lives an uneventful life in New York, where she works quietly as a hematology technician. She takes little active interest in parapsychology.

Monroe also warns that a hindering factor in the development of OBE abilities is the "fear barrier"—the student's own resistance to the experience. We all possess a certain inhibition about facing the unknown, and leaving the body is an experience we intuitively associate with either dying or going mad. We, therefore, have a natural fear of leaving the body deeply ingrained in us by our culture and society. Monroe admits that his own fear barrier lasted for several years, and that only after he conquered it could he fully explore his out-of-body potentials. It is just this barrier that keeps us in our bodies and represents the trickiest obstacle one must overcome before achieving the OBE. "I do not know how to circumvent the fear barrier," admits Monroe, "except by cautious initial steps to create familiarity bit by bit as you proceed."

Most of the great astral projectors of the past have written about something akin to the fear barrier. Forhan, in particular, notes the instinctive dread he felt any time something new and unexpected happened to him during his projections. Contacting a new dimension, confronting a disembodied entity for the first time, or having odd physical sensations all ignited this inherent trepidation. Gradually, however, he came to realize that the OBE world is primarily a mental one. Nothing could actually hurt him while he was out-of-body; it was his own fear that so often victimized him. He eventually discovered that he could change his environment and disperse any would-be astral attacker merely by an exercise of will. Once he learned this great secret, he never again worried about his well-being while out-of-body.

Perhaps this is a good lessson to learn *before* you try leaving the body. For practical purposes, the student should diligently study the literature on the OBEs before trying to project. The writings of the great astral projectors of yesteryear are especially good in this regard. They will prepare you for what you may experience while separated from your body. Had I known what I do today about the OBE, I do not think I would have been so uneasy about some of my initial experiences, such as the paralysis, the feeling of being sucked out of my body against my will, the vicious white faces I saw during one of my first incipient releases, and other encounters I had on the road to self-discovery.

Having psychologically prepared yourself for leaving the body, the steps described below may be implemented for inducing the experience.

Step one: Relax the body. According to Monroe, "the ability to relax is the first prerequisite, perhaps even the first step itself" to having an OBE. This includes both mental and physical relaxation. Although Monroe offers no specific exercises for relaxing, PMR or self-hypnosis will suffice.

Step two: Try to enter the state bordering sleep. Nearly all the great astral projectors have noted that the OBE seems related to that curious state right between waking and sleeping, known as the hypnagogic state. Dr. John Palmer found that his subjects at the University of Virginia who could enter an experimentally induced analog of this state (through ganzfeld stimulation) were the most successful at experiencing the OBE. This same finding has been made experientially, primarily by Sylvan Muldoon and Monroe himself.

Just how does one achieve this state voluntarily? The only way is through practice. When you lie down to sleep, observe the act of falling asleep. As you begin to doze off, try to hold your consciousness intact. At first you will lose your grip and fall asleep. Don't be discouraged. Eventually you will be able instinctively to judge when you are beginning to fall asleep. These cues will allow you to hold on to this twilight zone of consciousness indefinitely.

You can also use certain exercises to identify the hypnagogic state. I use a relatively simple one. When you lie down to sleep, hold a single mental image in your mind as long as you can. When *other* images start popping spontaneously into your mind, you have entered the hypnagogic state.

Learn to observe these images and passively study them. This process of observation will actually keep you awake, since the mind will be kept minimally stimulated but not actually aroused. I have used this technique for years and have even trained myself to observe these images, rouse myself, write them down, and then almost immediately return to the hypnagogic state. It is, indeed, all a matter of practice. Another old method of prolonging the hypnagogic state is to rest with your arm bent at the elbow and elevated. When you are just about to fall asleep, your arm will begin to fall and alert you to the fact. Again, with practice, you will eventually be able to hold that state right between waking and sleeping for a considerable period of time. The key is simply to become *aware* of it.

Monroe does not call this state by its formal psychological name; he simply calls it "Condition A."

Step three: Deepen the state. Monroe advises the student to learn how to deepen the hypnagogic state as a prerequisite to leaving the body. The first exercise is to learn how to clear the mind while remaining near sleep. "Do not think of anything, but remain posed between wakefulness and sleep," he advises. "Simply look through your closed eyelids at the blackness ahead of you. Do nothing more. After a number of these exercises, you may hallucinate 'mind pictures' or light patterns. These seem to have no great significance and may merely be forms of neural discharge."* When these images cease, one has entered what Monroe calls Condition B. From here one must learn to enter even deeper into Condition C—a state of such relaxation that one loses all awareness of the body and sensory stimulation. You are almost in a void in which your only source of stimulation will be your own thoughts.

The ideal state for leaving the body, however, is Condition D. This is the same as Condition C when it is voluntarily induced from a rested and refreshed condition and is not the result of the normal fatigue that brings on sleep. To achieve Condition D, Monroe suggests that you practice

*The "light patterns" one sees while entering sleep are technically called phosphenes and result when any stimulus other than light reaches the retina. They are not neural discharges, but purely optical effects.

entering it after you wake up in the morning or after a short nap. At that point you are refreshed, but still physically and mentally relaxed. Start the exercise before you begin moving about.

Although Monroe may disagree with me on this point, what he calls Conditions C and D may actually represent the first stage of actual sleep. It is hard to judge when a person slips from waking into true sleep. Subjects hooked to an EEG so that their brain waves can be monitored do not show a discrete changeover from a drowsy condition into sleep; the shift is very gradual. Individuals aroused during their initial light sleep may not even be aware that they have fallen under. They usually describe being preoccupied with their thoughts and do not recollect actually losing consciousness. Monroe seems to be teaching his students how to actually observe the process of waking-into-sleeping with no loss of consciousness. Psychologists now know that, even when we are not dreaming, our minds are occupied in constant mentation. So, Monroe's techniques may also be a systematic method for retaining some awareness of one's own thought processes during actual sleep onset.

Step four: Enter into a state of vibration. This is the most important part of Monroe's techniques, but it is also the most opaque.

Many people who have undergone an OBE have noted the curious "vibrations" that herald its onset. These vibrations can manifest in a variety of amplitudes, from a mild tingling sensation to the feeling that electricity is being shot through the body. Monroe experienced them for several weeks before having his first separation. Yet their cause remains a mystery. They may, indeed, be caused by the actual incipient release of the psychic double, or they may be the result of some sort of proprioceptive stimulation produced when one's normal body awareness is totally eliminated. Monroe does not claim that he knows what causes these curious vibrations, but he feels that producing them deliberately is the most critical step of all in inducing the OBE. For entering into this vibrational state as an adjunct to Condition D, he offers the following directions:

1. *Remove any and all jewelry or other accoutrements that might be touching your skin.*
2. *Darken the room so that no light can be seen through your eyelids, but do not shut out all light.*
3. *Lie down with your body along a north-south axis, with your head*

pointed toward magnetic north. (No reason is given for this specific position.)

4. *Loosen all clothing, but keep covered so that you are slightly warmer than might normally be comfortable.*

5. *Be sure you are in a location where, and at a time when, there will be absolutely no noise to disturb you.*

6. *Enter a state of deep relaxation.*

7. *Give yourself the mental suggestion that you will remember all that occurs during the upcoming session that will be beneficial to your well-being. Repeat this suggestion five times.*

8. *Proceed to breathe through your half-opened mouth.*

9. *As you breathe, concentrate on the void in front of you.*

10. *Select a point a foot away from your forehead, then change your point of mental reference to six feet.*

11. *Turn the point 90 degrees upward by drawing an imaginary line parallel to your body axis up and above your head. Focus there and reach out for the "vibrations" at that point and bring them back into your body.*

Exactly what are these "vibrations" that you are reaching for? And how do you bring them back into your head? Monroe is very vague on this issue, but he offers some information about what seems to be a way of mentally contacting them:

The only way to understand the vibrations is to experience them. Another way of making contact with the vibrations is by imagining that two lines are extending from your closed eyelids and converging about a foot or so away from your forehead. At the point where these two lines meet, try to experience a resistance or "pressure." You might imagine something like the sensation that would be experienced if poles of a magnet were forced together or if two electrical wires made contact. Proceed by extending this focal point about three feet away from you. As Monroe explains, "A compression of the space [forces?] between the converging lines must result, and the pressure must therefore increase to maintain the convergence." He goes on to suggest that you now extend the junction another three feet away, so that it rests at about a 30-degree angle from your head. Monroe suggests you even work out this angle with a protractor so that you can visualize it correctly. "Once," he continues, "you have learned to establish and maintain the 30-degree angle outward (or roughly six feet away), *send* the point of intersection 90-degrees (or in an 'L') upward in the direction of your head, but parallel to the axis of your body. You 'reach' with this point of intersection. Stretch or reach with the point more and more until you obtain a reaction."

Monroe asserts that you will know when a reaction has been reached. You will experience it as a surging, a hissing, or a pulsation inside the head. The vibrations will then surge through the entire body.

These are preliminary exercises, and Monroe assures the student that after due practice, he or she will be able to enter the state of vibration at will.

Step 5: Learn to control the vibrational state. After learning how to achieve this state, you must now begin exploring its many subtleties. Practice inducing the vibrations until you are no longer frightened by the waves and electrical feelings that accompany them. Monroe also suggests that you just relax and passively observe these vibrations until they are familiar to you. At that time you should practice controlling them by mentally pushing them into your head, down into your toes, making them surge throughout your entire body, and creating vibrational waves from head to foot. To produce this wave effect, concentrate on the vibrations and mentally "push" a wave out of the head and guide it down the body. Practice this procedure until you can induce these waves instantly on mental command. If the vibrations seem rough or shaky—remember that Bayless felt as if his body were being shaken by an earthquake—Monroe recommends that you mentally increase the vibrational rate. This will even them out.

Once you have control of the vibrational state, you are ready to actually leave the body.

Step 6: Begin with a partial separation. The key here is thought control. Keep your mind firmly focused on the idea of leaving the body. Do not let it wander. Stray thoughts may cause you to lose control of the state.

Now, having entered the vibrational state, begin exploring the OBE by releasing a hand or leg of the "second body." Monroe suggests that you stick your "hand" out as far as you can and touch a familiar object, such as a wall next to your bed. Then push a little more and allow your extremity to go through the object. Return the hand by placing it back into coincidence with your physical one, decrease your vibrational rate, and then terminate the experiment. Lie quietly until you have fully returned to normal. This exercise will prepare you for completely leaving the body.

Step 7: Dissociate yourself from the body. Monroe describes two basic techniques for implementing this ultimate separation. One method is to "lift out" of the body. To do so, think about getting lighter and lighter after you have entered the vibrational state. Think how nice it would be to float upward. Keep this thought in mind at all costs and let no extraneous thoughts interrupt it. An OBE will occur naturally at this point.

Another method Monroe uses for leaving the body is the "rotation method" or "roll-out" technique. When you have achieved the vibrational state, try to roll over as if you were turning over in bed. Do not attempt to turn over physically by moving your arms or legs. Try to twist your body from the top and virtually roll over in your second body right out of your physical self. At this point you will be out-of-body but next to it. Think of floating upward, and you should find yourself floating above your body.

Monroe recommends beginning with the lift-out method, but argues that both procedures will be equally efficacious for inducing a total separation.

Monroe also offers several suggestions for experiments and exercises that you may wish to try once you have left the body. These experiments will not concern us here, and Monroe's book may be consulted for further details. It is also suggested that one should become familiar with the feeling of being out-of-body before making any further explorations. During first trials, the student should not attempt to leave the room in which he or she is projecting.

COMMENTS

When evaluating the Monroe techniques, the main thing to keep in mind is that they are *personal* procedures. Monroe developed them from his own experiences; they may work for him, but they may not necessarily work for anyone else.

His assurances about the universal viability of the "roll-out" method is a good case in point. My own OBEs are usually heralded by what Monroe calls the vibrational state, although this state usually manifests itself spontaneously. I have little control over it and often have difficulty getting out of the body at this point. This is especially true if I cannot focus my concentration long enough on the feeling of being fully separated from my body. Sometimes I will even get halfway out, but remain partially stuck back in the physical! (Once I got stuck with my head and upper torso out of the body, but with the rest of me, from the waist down, fully coincident with my physical self. The next day I woke up with a slender line of pain all around my waist where the juncture had existed the night before.) I found that the best way to leave the body at this point was a "lift-out" procedure, although I made this discovery long before Monroe published his autobiography. After reading *Journeys Out of the Body*, however, I tried experimenting with the roll-out procedure, but I never had any luck with it. I have, indeed, felt the curious sensation of actually rolling over and over within my body, but I have never been able actually to roll out of it.

The message here is simple. What holds true for one person will not necessarily hold true for everyone. Leaving the body is a very personal matter, and individual differences obviously play an important part in developing the skill.

On the other hand, one of the main virtues of Monroe's techniques is the concentration on the vibrational state. This state is universally described by astral projectors, yet no one has ever written anything about its nature or how to induce it. John Palmer attempted to imitate this sensation during his University of Virginia project. He had his volunteer subjects try to induce OBEs while they sat in a vibrating chair, and had some success with the procedure. Yet even this work reveals nothing about why or how these vibrations are linked to the OBE. Monroe's writings on the subject are, therefore, potentially very important.

It is here, unfortunately, that the Monroe techniques become rather obscure. His elaborate method of reaching out and mentally grabbing vibrations from the air seems arbitrary and without any coherent rationale.

But the real question at issue is rather simple. Has Monroe actually been able to induce OBEs through his own methods? He has participated in at least two major experimental projects during which his OBEs have been monitored under controlled conditions. These tests were conducted at the University of Virginia by Dr. Charles Tart and at the Topeka V.A. Hospital by Drs. Stuart Twemlow and Fowler Jones, who recently initiated an ambitious research program into the nature of the OBE. The results of these experiments are crucial in judging Monroe's credibility—more so since he later bowed out, under highly suspicious circumstances, of a similar experiment scheduled at the University of Virginia in the early 1970s.

Dr. Tart initiated his tests after he met Monroe in 1965. Tart was a psychologist at the University of Virginia at the time and had access to a psychophysiology laboratory at the University hospital. Monroe participated in nine experiments from December 1965 to August 1966. The tests were all basically run the same way. Monroe was placed in a room of the lab that was equipped with a cot, where he could lie down and spend the night. Electrodes were attached to his head and chest, which led to a polygraph in an adjoining equipment room where Tart (or an assistant) could monitor his brain waves, heartbeat, and other physiological functions. Monroe was merely requested to settle down to sleep, leave the body, float out of the sleep chamber, and into the equipment room. A five-digit number was placed on a shelf located there. His next task was to look at the number, return to his body, and report the number back to the experimenters.

Although Monroe was never able to succeed at this experiment,* there were some surprises in store for everyone. During his eighth night at the lab, Monroe managed to induce two OBEs. After settling down, he was able to roll out of his body, float near his cot, and leave the sleep chamber. He found himself in an unknown room, presumably in the hospital, where two people were talking. When he found that he could not attract their attention, he returned to his body. Returning to the sleep chamber helped to orientate him, and he initiated a second OBE. This time he left the sleep chamber and entered the equipment room, but he was surprised to see that no one was there. He searched around a bit and found Dr. Tart's assistant in the corridor talking to a man. Monroe tried to get their attention, and the assistant seemed to respond. He was not able to get the man's attention, however, so he once again returned to his body.

Monroe later learned that his observations had been correct. Tart's assistant had left the room at one point during the experiment when her husband had called on her. She had gone out into the corridor to talk to him.

*While working at the University of California at Davis, Tart met and worked with another subject who eventually succeeded.

Dr. Tart was also intrigued by Monroe's psychophysiology. His OBEs appeared to manifest during a poorly defined dream state.

When Tart moved to the University of California at Davis, work with Monroe was resumed. The psychologist managed to get Monroe there for only one night in 1968. This test was designed along similar lines to the Virginia project. Monroe spent the night in a University lab room equipped with a comfortable bed and polygraph leads. He was able to induce an OBE that night, but could not manage to get into the adjoining room where a target number had been placed on a shelf. He apparently got lost after leaving the body, traveled in the wrong direction, and ended up in a courtyard next to the lab. When he realized that he had lost his way, he returned to the body. The experiment was technically a failure, but Monroe was able to correctly describe the courtyard nonetheless, although he had never visited it before.

The readouts on his psychophysiology were also interesting. The OBE had occurred during an initial sleep state marked by a sudden drop in his blood pressure. The records indicated that he was not dreaming, however.

Tart also designed some tests to see if Monroe could project from Virginia to his own residence in Berkeley. The results were inconclusive.

Monroe later submitted to tests at the Topeka V.A. Hospital in Kansas. There his OBE talents were studied by Stuart Twemlow and Fowler Jones. The crux of the project was to assess Monroe's personality profile, in hope of finding any clues that might relate to his OBEs. The doctors were also able to run a few psychophysiological tests with their subject. Monroe was placed in one room of the hospital's psychophysiology lab, where he was instructed to induce an OBE and then signal the experimenters over an intercom upon his return. A technician was stationed in an adjoining room to monitor the equipment, while Twemlow and Jones watched Monroe through a one-way window from yet a third location. When Monroe began inducing his OBE, they were in for quite a surprise.

"At about the same time as a technician entered the room to tell us that the brain-wave tracings were changing," writes Twemlow, "Dr. Jones and I simultaneously had the impression of a heatwavelike distortion of Monroe's upper body, while the lower part of his body was clearly in focus to us. This distortion lasted until approximately two minutes before the termination of the experiment.''

The researchers later learned that Monroe's self-reported OBE coincided with the observable changes in his brain-wave readings.

In general, the Kansas researchers found that Monroe's OBEs were accompanied by a rather discrete brain state in which his brain waves slowed down and became less varied. They maintain that Monroe was actually able to alter his brain state into a narrow frequency band in order to leave the body.

All these tests and data are certainly suggestive, but this is not to say that Monroe's credibility is unimpeachable. Strong experimental evidence certainly does exist to show that he can leave the body, but many of Monroe's other claims remain somewhat questionable.

In his autobiography, for instance, Monroe claims that his initial OBEs were related to curious attacks of cramps and vibrations. Yet several years earlier he had written an account of his experiences under the pseudonymn of Bob Rame. It was published in 1962 by Dr. Andrija Puharich, a maverick researcher from California, as a chapter in his book, *Beyond Telepathy*. Most of the accounts—Monroe's and Rame's—are identical, except that in his Rame accounts Monroe admits that his first OBEs were deliberately induced by glue-sniffing. Perhaps Monroe simply did not wish to do anything to promote this dangerous practice when he set about writing his book. (Little was known about glue sniffing in the 1950s.) But Monroe was not too wise to leave this discrepancy in print.

Monroe's credibility has also been more seriously questioned when David Black, an investigative reporter from the East, decided to check up on *Journeys Out of the Body* in 1973. Black could not locate any of the people Monroe mentions in his book who could corroborate his OBE visitations, and he found the Virginia businessman evasive when questioned about the matter.

My own opinion is that Monroe probably does have the ability to leave his body, but has exaggerated and romanticized his accounts. His writings about the OBE certainly contain much understanding and insight about the experience, leading me to believe that he has much personal knowledge of it. But how much and to what extent must remain a mystery.

The fact that Monroe's first OBEs were induced by glue-sniffing should not detract from the validity of his experiences, however. Artificial means for leaving the body are numerous. People who have experimented with marijuana, LSD, and MDA (3,4 methylene-dioxy amphetamine) have reported spontaneous OBEs, and there seems no reason not to take these accounts at face value. However, one must remember that the OBE induction methods Monroe outlines were developed by someone who had already induced the experiences via a very different, and potentially dangerous, means. They may, therefore, be more suited for someone who has already had a few previous OBEs than for someone wishing to develop the skill from scratch.

Apart from his personal techniques, Monroe founded and opened his own institute in the 1970s to help the general public explore the OBE state. His institute is located in Faber, Virginia, where workshops are held and new methods of self-exploration are being developed.*

The basic goal of the institute is to help the client explore his or her inner self. It is not focused on the OBE per se, although the induction of an OBE is part of the overall program taught there. A client who enrolls in the Gateway program, the featured attraction, spends a week at the center's headquarters. The program includes several sessions in an isolation booth where he or she is fitted with a headset and listens to specially prepared tapes. There are taped procedures for relaxation, control of the body's energy systems, exploring alternate realities, and experiencing the OBE.

The aim of these tapes, a mixture of pulsating wave sounds and verbal instructions, is to synchronize the hemispheres of the brain. The brain is divided into two hemispheres, each in charge of certain functions. It is generally maintained that the left controls logical and analytical functions, while the right regulates spacial and aesthetic tasks. Each hemisphere puts out a continuous series of electrical impulses, which can be monitored by an electroencephalograph. It is quite normal for the two hemispheres to be out of synchronization. Monroe and the Institute claim that their tapes synchronize the electrical activity of the hemispheres, allowing the client to explore his or her inner self more easily and without resistance from the brain.

This is, of course, only a very brief and cursory summary of the Institute's program. Whether it actually works is a different matter.

*The mailing address of the Monroe Institute of Applied Sciences is P.O. Box 94C, Faber, Virginia 22938. I would like to thank the staff of the Institute for supplying me with some of the following material. This does not mean, however, that I necessarily endorse the Institute's programs.

Some people obviously benefit greatly from the program. One prominent supporter is Dr. Elizabeth Kubler-Ross, the well-known authority on death and dying, who visited the Institute in hopes of experiencing an OBE. She wanted to know what it actually felt like to "die" (leave the body) so that she could better understand her fatally ill patients. Her enthusiastic endorsement of the Institute appeared as part of a February 1980 *Cosmopolitan* magazine interview. Not only did Kubler-Ross have a classic OBE during one of her initial sessions, but after another of her sessions underwent what psychologists call a "peak" experience—where one seems joyfully to merge with all of creation.

And Dr. Kubler-Ross certainly is not alone in her enthusiasm. Writing in a recent issue of *Fate* magazine, former California TV writer James Bryce tells of his own awesome reactions to the Gateway program. He apparently did not have a classic OBE during his stay, but reminds his readers that "participation in a Monroe Institute seminar should not be considered if your main goal is to have an OBE. That's not what the program is about. It is about changing your views of reality to such a degree that you no longer merely wonder about those 'special' extra senses but begin to use them in a way that improves your life." He adds that "the research at the Institute has provided a tool which allows people to explore the outer reaches of consciousness and bring back information and guidance to enhance their personal lives and to help create their own reality." Bryce does not mention, however, that the OBE is an integral part of the Institute's concentration. A tape meant to help the client explore the OBE is even included in the guidance manual sent to people preparing to participate in one of the programs. A bulletin sent to me from the Monroe Institute goes on to stress that the purpose of the Gateway program is to, in part, ". . .achieve and willfully control his physical body and the out-of-body state, communicate with and visit other energy structures and realities." So, the Gateway experience must be considered essentially an out-of-body induction procedure.

Should the Institute's Gateway program be considered a particularly viable approach to exploring the OBE?

Despite the enthusiastic support of Kulber-Ross and others, several criticisms could be leveled at the Institute and its programs. Although the center offers a wide variety of programs and activities, it often displays a very naive understanding of psychophysiology and psychobiology. A small booklet distributed by the center and entitled *Brain Power* points out the differences between the functions of the brain's hemispheres, but fails to mention that discrete lateralization functions generally hold true only for right-handed individuals, not for many left handers. Nor is there any reason to believe that the HEMI-SYNC tapes can really help induce the OBE. Several successful attempts have been made to monitor the brain waves of people undergoing the OBE, and the data obtained from these studies do not indicate that hemispheric synchonization is a consistent or even indicative feature of the experience. Nor is everybody who goes through the program invariably pleased with it.

S. Keith Harary, himself a gifted OBE subject, underwent an earlier version of the current program and considered it useless as a viable approach to the OBE. And I once received a letter from a couple who had taken the Gateway program and who felt they had been ripped off by the Institute. Since I was a consulting editor for a nationwide psychic magazine, they were writing to me, they explained, in the hope that I could advise them how they could best warn the public against what they considered consumer fraud.

Since I have never gone through the Gateway program and do not plan to, I can neither recommend nor criticize it. It appears obvious that the procedures used there, *as with all of the techniques outlined in this book*, will work for some individuals but not for others. One's sensitivity to altered states of consciousness, willingness, and readiness to have an OBE, and previous experience with self-exploration techniques, will all play a role in how one reacts to the Gateway program. None of the literature I have seen from the Institute guarantees that the client will have an OBE just by taking part in the program, so Monroe and his staff are certainly not guilty of false advertising or superhype. Yet it seems to me that there are simpler—and cheaper—ways of getting to the heart of the OBE. Participation in an Institute program is not exactly inexpensive, and a membership in the Institute costs $155, of which $60 may be deducted from the registration fees for any one of their programs. Taped programs for home use are also available.

If willingness and desire to have an OBE are the keys to this strange phenomenon, then perhaps the Gateway seminar really will help many people. Other students and inquirers might not find the week-long program suited to their temperament.

REFERENCES

Black, David. *Ekstacy: Out-of-the-Body Experiences*. New York: Bobbs-Merrill, 1975.

Bryce, James. The man who journeys afar. *Fate*, August, 1982.

Monroe, Robert. *Journeys Out of the Body*. Garden City, N.Y.: Double-day, 1962.

Puharich, Andrija. *Beyond Telepathy*. Garden City, N.Y.: Doubleday, 1962.

Tart, Charles. A second psychophysiological study of out-of-the-body experiences in a gifted subject. *International Journal of Parapsychology*, 1967, *9*, pp. 251-58.

_____ . Introduction to Robert Monroe's *Journeys Out of the Body*, op. cit.

Twemlow, Stuart. Epilogue: personality file. In Robert Monroe, *Journeys Out of the Body*. Garden City, N.Y.: Anchor/Doubleday, 1977 (updated edition).

chapter seven
Projection Through Visualization

Most systems for out-of-body travel recognize the crucial role played by visualization. Lancelin recommended visualization as a method for directing the out-of-body voyager to a desired location or friend; while Muldoon suggested visualizing one's self in a mirror and then merging with it to induce the experience. Both the Tibetan yogis and Minnie Keeler's "communicators" listed scores of visualization techniques designed to help the student leave the body, and even the Jewish Cabalists realized the great power of mental imagery. It should not be surprising, therefore, that whole systems for leaving the body have been based on this process.

BACKGROUND

Visualization and mental imagery are great psychological enigmas. We know relatively little about the mind's inner pictures, yet the power of mental imagery has been known for centuries. The ancient Egyptians believed that images held in the mind could materially affect the physical universe and that one could bring about a desired event merely by visualizing it. Hermetic magic, which developed around the philosophy and occult teachings of the Egyptian teacher Hermes Trismegistus, contended that thoughts contained physical properties and that, by manipulating them, one could control the world. It was also believed that spiritual development was inherently related to mental imagery and the uses one could make of it. Another old occult belief was that by holding a mental image in mind, you became imbued by the qualities of the visualized object.

Parapsychologists today have learned that imagery strategies can help people gain access to their ESP powers, and even produce mind-over-matter effects. Many psychics use visualization techniques to "look" into sealed boxes and perform other tasks, while other gifted subjects can move objects by willfully visualizing the act. So, there might be a grain of at least psychological truth in these old beliefs.

Ritual visualization plays a prime role in Christian contemplation as well as in the art of the primitive shaman. The shamans were (and are) the wonder-workers and healers of many technologically undeveloped cultures. When asked to heal a sick patient, they undergo a mental journey in which they visualize themselves traveling to other worlds, finding the patient's soul, and returning it to his or her body. In fact, the use of visualization as a means of self-learning and psychological transcendence plays a role in just about all religions and in all world cultures. The art and practice of visualization reached its zenith in the tantric yoga of Tibet, where specific exercises for developing imagery skills are outlined in great depth. Even in our own technological society, medicine and psychology are learning about the power of mental imagery. Evidence now exists that such diseases as cancer can be treated and fought by the use of imagery strategies.

An interesting connection also exists between visualization, the spiritual path, and the OBE. Most mystical traditions rely on the creative power of visualization for both leaving the body and attaining spiritual transcendence. Cabalism in particular teaches the student to envision a complex cosmological diagram called the "Tree of Life" until he or she sees the meaning behind it. This insight purportedly allows the individual to "see" (in the mind's eye) the realities of the spiritual world. Cabalism also teaches that this type of deep contemplation may lead to a form of OBE. If one focuses on the images of the Hebrew characters long enough, writes the great Jewish scholar G. Scholem, the student may "see the shape of his self standing before him and he forgets his self and it is disengaged from him and he sees the shape of the self before him talking to him and predicting the future." A bright light will then encompass him and he will experience union with God.

This is, of course, very similar to what people who have had near-death encounters—vivid OBEs at the moment of clinical death—have reported. Many people revived from clinical death relate how they left their bodies, entered a great white or golden light, and sometimes even saw pictures or revelations of the future. Dr. Kenneth Ring of the University of Connecticut at Storrs is studying this phenomenon. These parallels suggest that some forms of Cabalistic visualiztion were meant to induce a form of near-death (OBE) experience.

Nor is conventional Roman Catholicism immune from teachings about visualization and the OBE. St. Ignatius of Syria wrote a spiritual manual in the first century A.D. in which he advocated visualizing holy scenes as a means for achieving ecstasy. The term *ecstasy* has had a rather troubled history in Catholic thought, and for years a debate raged as to whether spiritual ecstasy entailed the release of the soul from the body.

Tantric yoga also possesses a curious method of inducing the OBE through visualization as a means of understanding the nature of the self and the world. The student is instructed to stare into a mirror on which the figure of a female deity has been painted. He is told to use powers of visualization to animate what he or she sees in the mirror. The image of the self can be used. With proper practice it will become real and independent; eventually becoming animate in the space between the mirror and the viewer. This exercise is essentially a spiritual one, however, since its purpose is to take the student out of the physical world and show him or her the objective reality of the mental realm where the yogi can liberate himself from all worldly desires.

All of these procedures seem to be pointing in the same direction. The process of visualization makes us forget our bodies. It allows the mind to become independent of the burden of the flesh and its material world. This disembodied state then permits the student to better explore the nature of spiritual reality and learn from it.

THE TECHNIQUES

Visualization may lead to a different kind of OBE than we have been discussing. Virtually all of the induction methods surveyed so far have been based on the assumption that astral projection entails the release of some sort of "soul vehicle" from the physical body—the so-called astral body about which Muldoon wrote so much, the phantom double of the French fluidists, the etheric body of the occultists, and so on. Yet, many people who undergo spontaneous OBEs do not perceive themselves as anything like such a form.

For instance, during the course of her case collecting, Celia Green found that 80 percent of her correspondents described themselves as being *totally* disembodied while out-of-body. This finding has been confirmed by Dr. Susan Blackmore of the University of Bristol in England. She polled 172 students at the University of Amsterdam about any OBEs they might have had. While 34 students reported affirmatively, only four had perceived themselves as occupying a phantom body during the experience. Most described how they merely floated about as a point in space, were contained within only a vague amorphous shape of some sort, or had no awareness of how they were traveling. These data may indicate that the acronym "OBE" is actually a generic term under which we have been placing many different phenomena. There may, indeed, be different forms of the OBE. One may entail the release of a soul body, while the other may be the simple release of consciousness.

The phenomenon of disembodied traveling has also led some authorities to believe that the OBE experience is not really the release of consciousness from the body, but a form of perceptual anomaly in which some aspect of the perceiving self momentarily views the environment from a perspective other than the physical body. They argue that the OBE is, therefore, a perceptual illusion and not a genuine psychic phenomenon. This issue is, of course, moot.

Whatever the case, visualization exercises may be the key to this curious form of the OBE. Such an experience would certainly be normally classified as an OBE, since the consciousness would be experienced as free-floating in space and would be capable of making detailed observations from that perspective.

Various formal procedures for leaving the body through visualization strategies have come to us from numerous sources. The key ingredient in most of them is simple. You must learn how to visualize your whereabouts from a perspective independent of the body. This strategy is to be practiced until you can shift the focus of your awareness out of the body at will. One simple procedure, currently taught by many so-called mind dynamics outfits, is as follows:

1. *Select a room where you will be undisturbed while you practice.*
2. *Sit in a comfortable chair facing either a bare wall or some sort of blank visual field. Staring at a blank motion picture screen or a white sheet draped over an entryway will suffice.*
3. *The view should be unobstructed, so move any furniture or other objects out of your peripheral view.*
4. *Place a simple object—a vase, book, ashtray, or whatever—directly in front of your line of vision. The blank wall will serve as a backdrop. The object should be simple in design, with as little decoration as possible.*
5. *Stare at the object until you have virtually memorized everything about it, including shape, design, color, and contours.*
6. *Close your eyes and visualize the object and the room itself. Do not merely imagine all this, but recreate the room and the object in your mind's eye in proper perspective and proportion.*
7. *Do not imagine the mentally created room "in your head" so to speak, but "out there" just as though you had X-ray vision and were seeing it through your closed eyelids.*
8. *As soon as the image fades or you cannot hold it any longer, open your eyes and refresh your memory about what the room looks like.*
9. *Repeat the process.*

This is your preliminary exercise. You might begin by practicing it every day for 15 or 20 minutes. The key is to do this each day without fail. Once you have mastered the exercise, you can go on to the next phase of the program.

1. *Repeat the above process with a clock in front of you. Memorize the time.*
2. *Close your eyes and visualize the clock.*
3. *Watch your mental clock tick away.*
4. *After several minutes, open your eyes and check the time on the real dial. If the time is roughly the same, your power of visualization is rising to its peak.*

What does all of this have to do with leaving the body? The answer is that you will be gradually learning to project some aspect of your mind away from the body. By practicing how to create a mental replica of the world with which you can perceptually interact, you are learning to make a jump from the real world to a mentally constructed one.

If you practice hard and long enough, this type of perceptual jump may begin to occur spontaneously. This phenomenon will be experienced as an OBE. Steve Richards, a student and writer on yoga now living in Texas, has specifically written on the power that this exercise has for inducing spontaneous OBEs. "After two weeks of this kind of practice," he writes, "you may start having some spontaneous astral projection experiences. Don't expect too much at first. . .But if you persist you may find some evening as you are dropping off to sleep that you have the experience of 'stepping out' of your body just before you lose consciousness. These experiences will come most frequently in the late evening and in the very early morning."

In other words, the above exercises help train the mind to function independently of the cues we pick up about our environment through our senses. The mind then begins to function perceptually without any reliance on these organs—and that entails an OBE.

During your self-training, you may undergo some curious experiences that will help you to know when you are on the right track. While visualizing, you might be unable for a moment to tell whether your eyes are open or closed. When you are about to go to sleep, you may suddenly find that you are seeing your room clearly, even though your eyes are closed. This very revealing experience indicates that the mind has begun to function at a perceptual level beyond normal sight. If and when this happens, try willing your consciousness to leave the body. It probably will.

Practically all the great astral projectors of the past have experienced this peculiar phenomenon. As an OBE begins to manifest, but before the consciousness has left the body, the individual will occasionally see the room clearly, though his or her eyes will remain closed. The room will be quite visible and sometimes even more illuminated than it "really" is.

Whether such an OBE is real or a trick of the imagination is really not the point. Remember that the term "out-of-body experience" is only a descriptive label. It is not an explanation for the experience of leaving the body, nor does it imply one. Even most parapsychologists are uncertain whether the mind actually leaves the body during the experience. Some researchers believe that a definite aspect of the mind really does separate from the body. Both Dr. Tart and myself hold this basic view. Yet many other researchers, such as Susan Blackmore and John Palmer, believe that the OBE is really a quirk of mental imagery. So, whether one particular "type" of OBE is any more of a mind/body separation than any other is rather question-begging. Any experience during which a person finds him- or herself viewing the environment from a point *other* than the physical body is a valid OBE. What specific form the experience takes is not a pertinent issue. In the Comments section below, however, I cite evidence that projectors who produce OBEs through intense visualization are able to make veridical observations about distant places and events. This alone would indicate that visualization is a valid road to the OBE and that visualized OBEs may be just as valid as any other.

The above exercises are meant basically to incite spontaneous OBEs. Other exercises have been developed to induce and control the experience more dynamically. A complete system for OBE training and travel has been developed by Richard Greene of Cambridge, Massachusetts, who published his program in a privately printed monograph. This empirically based system has evolved partially through Greene's work with several willing students. The following steps for inducing the OBE have been summarized from Greene's own much more elaborate descriptions and discussions. Note how his procedures are basically extensions of the imagery strategies discussed above.

Step 1: Develop the ability to activate the imagination. Since visualization is the key to the Greene system, the student must first learn to construct and control mental images. The basic procedure is to learn how to hold simple mental images in the mind and sustain them. Anyone can conjure up a picture in the mind, but it takes practice to hold it there without it either dissolving or being replaced by intruding ones. Greene recommends beginning with certain occult symbols, such as a red equilateral triangle, a blue circle, a black oval, a yellow square, or a white crescent. Sit in a quiet place, select one of these symbols, and practice holding it in your mind's eye. You will have achieved your goal when you can hold the image for 10 minutes without losing it. Practice often, but use a different symbol for each session so that you do not become dependent on any particular image. Practice daily for at least 10 minutes.

Step 2. Learn correct breathing as an adjunct to the exercise. Here, Greene draws from the yogic tradition summarized in Chapter 5. He recommends a simplified method of pranayama in which one inhales to the count of five, holds for six, and exhales while counting to four. The breath is kept out until the count of six; then the student initiates the next cycle. Greene argues (based on yogic cosmology) that this breathing technique energizes the body and helps the consciousness acquire enough energy to leave the body. It is not totally clear from his writings whether you should practice the breathing while learning to visualize or practice it independently. At some point, however, you should integrate the two practices. Greene specifically emphasizes that you should exercise daily and especially when you feel drained or tired. This will keep the system energized and the body ready for the release of consciousness.

Step 3: Learn to transfer your consciousness into an inanimate object. To learn this skill—a favorite taught by many "mind dynamics" groups—place a cup or other simple object across the room from where you are sitting. You may sit with your eyes open or closed. Concentrate on the object, and try to merge with it until you actually become one with it. The identification should be so complete that you experience yourself *as* the cup.

This really is not as difficult as it may sound. By focusing your whole attention on the object, you will eventually find that your perception of the room and even your own body will momentarily blur. This is a good sign, so keep practicing until your only conscious awareness is of the object and your own mind. By continual practice you will find that you will not be able to differentiate yourself from the object you are focusing on. This exercise is also taught in some schools of Buddhism. It is meant to show the student that we perceive ourselves as independent from our environment only out of habit and false (categorical) thinking.

Once you have achieved this level of fusion, observe the room from the perspective of the object, that is, from the other side of the room. You should even be able to see your physical body sitting across from you. Greene recommends that you practice this skill every day for five to 10 minutes. Exercise until you can switch your mind to the independent perspective at will. This in itself is a limited form of OBE.

Step 4: Learn to project your consciousness away from the body to any perspective you choose. You might begin by transferring your consciousness out of the body to the other side of the room. This imagery exercise is virtually identical to what you learned in Step 3, but in this case you are doing away with using a focal object as a crutch. Greene notes that "many of your thoughts and ideas should now stem from where your mental consciousness is now placed. You should be able to think from that spot. You should also feel as if you are really located where the mental consciousness is." Greene calls this phenomenon "mental traveling," and it is very similar to what the old-time mesmerists called traveling clair-voyance. Once you have accomplished this transference of consciousness, you can terminate the session by willing your consciousness back to your physical body.

Greene warns that while practicing this exercise, you may retain awareness of your body. This does not necessarily mean you have failed, but that only a part of your awareness is functioning away from the body. You might also feel as though your awareness is bouncing back and forth between the two locations. This may be caused through force of habit. It will take time, and at first your awareness will have a natural resistance to functioning outside of the body's normal perspective.

Step 5. Practice projecting the mind totally away from the body. Begin by sitting or lying down as usual. Clear your mind of all extraneous thoughts, and practice the rhythmic breathing techniques outlined in Step 2. Visualize your body surrounded by an oval shell of light. (You might also visualize your body surrounded by your soul body.) Now visualize this vehicle floating up and away from the physical. To return, you need only visualize the phantom body returning to its physical home, or you need only will it to return. Re-entry will probably be spontaneous.

This step may actually be superfluous to learning out-of-body skills. By mastering Step 4, you have already achieved a form of OBE, although you might still be wondering if you are actually leaving the body during these mind-traveling experiences or are only deluding yourself. If you still have doubts, you may want to document this form of the OBE objectively. Although Greene does not give much advice on the matter, OBEs pro-duced through visualized mind traveling can easily be confirmed. You might ask a friend to write out and place a three-digit number on a shelf in the room you use for your practice sessions. The shelf should, of course, be out of your normal visual range. After you have transferred your aware-ness away from the body, see if you can float over and read it. If you succeed, you have achieved your goal!

Greene's handbook also includes discussions on problems you may face while leaving the body, how to achieve "peak" experiences, advice on experiments you might wish to try with your environment, how belief systems can influence your experiences, and so on. These issues will not concern us here, and Greene's own writings may be consulted for further information.*

Visualization techniques were also taught by many of the "occult societies" that flourished in England at the turn of the century, such as the famous Order of the Golden Dawn and its many offshoots. These techniques were basically simple visualization strategies similar to the ones discussed in this chapter, but often mixed in with the execution of occult rituals, including evocations and symbolic rites. While giving the student a great sense of self-importance, these rituals probably had no bearing on the ability to leave the body. They served only to help focus on the task at hand. Other "secret" occult techniques of the Victorian Age relied on highly specific visualization strategies; some are interesting and deserve special comment, even though many academic parapsychologists might disdain them.

It is quite fashionable for parapsychologists today to look askance at anything smacking of the "occult." It is sadly true that much traditional occultism is an odd assortment of superstition, meaningless ritual, and just plain nonsense. Yet, the practitioners of ritual magic and formal occultism were often intelligent people capable of making great discoveries and insights about the spiritual path and the world. The legacy of the great occultists contains genuine pearls of wisdom. The societies founded on their teachings were interested in the practical application of psychic powers, an issue that parapsychology today is only now beginning to address. What traditional occultism teaches us about the actual *practice* of psychic ability is often illuminating and may potentially be very important to modern researchers. This is especially true of astral projection, a favorite topic and practice among occultists.

Most of these occult teachings advise the student to develop intense imagery skills before using visualization for actually leaving the body. Specific exercises include visualizing a room with your eyes closed until every single detail can be recreated in the mind, looking at a picture and then recreating it in the mind over and over until every shade and constituent of the picture can be mentally experienced, and staring at a three-dimensional object and then mentally walking around it and experiencing

*Greene's The Handbook of Astral Projection may be ordered directly from Stellar Communications, P.O. Box 1403, Nashua, NH 03063.

it from various perspectives. Once the initiate mastered these practices, specific exercises for leaving the body were taught. It was stressed, however, that an OBE would take place only when and if the mind were ready to experience it. Several visualization strategies were meant to trigger the OBE rather than actually to induce it.

One common technique was to have the student sit in a semidarkened room, close the eyes, and imagine him- or herself sitting in a distant corner. Another method entailed sitting the student in a chair, eyes closed, and instructing him or her to visualize a duplicate "self" seated right in front. Then the student was to experience him- or herself moving forward and merging with his or her "double." Still a third technique taught the neophyte to lie down and visualize him- or herself rising into the air until all awareness of the bed was lost. At this point the student was instructed to visualize standing at the foot of the bed watching him- or herself. Each technique was to be practiced over and over until the student felt as though he or she were actually (that is, physically) participating in his or her visualizations.

Aleister Crowley, the famous "black magician" of England, taught a similar exercise briefly described earlier in this book. He had his students visualize a shut door set within a blank wall. A symbol or glyph that the student had already used as a meditational aid was to be imagined on the door. The student was to visualize the door opening slowly and him- or herself moving through it. This exercise was to be practiced over and over until the student actually projected right out of the body. At least one modern student and scholar of the occult, British author Kenneth Grant, believes that he once contacted a whole new level of reality through an OBE that he spontaneously experienced while practicing this exercise.

Most occult techniques for inducing the OBE rely on practicing a transference of consciousness experience similar to the ones Greene and others like him have more formally codified and stripped of their arcane trappings.

The nineteenth-century occultists were, however, a bit more sophisticated about the OBE than some groups and teachers who currently advocate these visualization strategies. They believed that these visualization exercises created mock forms of the experience, which, with constant practice, would ignite a genuine OBE when the student was prepared for it. In other words, you were told to practice leaving the body until it actually happened! These repetitions probably helped focus the student's will on the desire to have an OBE until the suggestion finally took hold at an unconscious level. Or they may have been ways of training the mind to overcome its natural resistance toward leaving the body.

COMMENTS

These procedures may sound absurdly simple—but no one ever claimed that astral projection was necessarily difficult. The basic idea behind these techniques seems to be that by practicing the experience of leaving the body, it will eventually happen. Another way of looking at the issue is that you are training yourself to make a perceptual jump from one point of observation to another. Dr. Susan Blackmore makes an analogy between the OBE and the type of perceptual jump that occurs when you stare at the Necker cube, a paradoxical shape that seems suddenly to shift its structure.

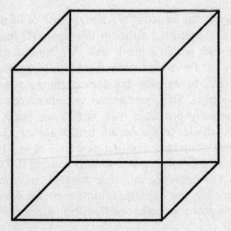

Notice how the cube seems to change as you stare at it. You can sometimes even induce the perceptual jump merely by blinking your eyes. Some parapsychologists believe that the OBE is, in fact, a quirk of perception analogous to this phenomenon. The perceptual jump model is not necessarily purely psychological, however. Such changes in orientation may be a quirk of perception, or they may actually represent the sudden physical dislocation of awareness to a point outside the body.

S. Keith Harary likes to make a challenging little point pertinent to this idea. When talking about his OBEs, he reminds his listeners that there really is no evidence that "awareness" is in the body in the first place. There is really no evidence that it is "contained" in the brain. Awareness is not physical at all; it is totally nonmaterial. It therefore can't be contained "in" anything. We probably *experience* it within our heads from habit. Our job is to learn to break this habit, and if we can, we can experience our awareness anywhere. And that is just what Harary believes an OBE entails.

The visualization exercises discussed here might well be perfect ways to prepare the mind for these jumps in orientation. They may begin to occur gradually as one practices over a period of time, or perhaps spontaneously as an outgrowth of the training. Such instances of mind travel would probably not entail the release of a soul body, but would manifest as sudden and instantaneous withdrawals of the consciousness from the body.

At least one noted psychic habitually relies on a form of visualization-cum-mind-travel for experiencing an OBE. Ingo Swann is a New York artist and psychic whose OBE talents were tested by the American Society for Psychical Research in 1971. Janet Mitchell, a research assistant at the A.S.P.R. at the time, was in charge of running the tests. The design of the experiment was simple, but it eventually revealed quite a bit about the OBE. A special lab room at the A.S.P.R. was outfitted with a boxlike shelf suspended under the ceiling. The shelf was illuminated by a light bulb so that any object placed in it could be seen clearly. Since Swann induces his OBEs from a waking state, he would not have to make elaborate preparations for them. He would merely sit in an easy chair under the shelf while polygraph electrodes were attached to his head. Swann would then liberate a part of his mind, send it up to the ceiling, see what pictures had been placed there, and simultaneously report what he was seeing to his experimenter.

Swann is a gifted artist so he also usually drew sketches of what he saw. Sometimes these sketches were identical to the target pictures placed on the shelf. What was even more intriguing was the *way* Swann saw the targets. His OBE vision seemed to be regulated by certain principles, just as physical sight adheres to the laws of optics. His results certainly did not seem to resemble the fragmented, symbolized, and "global" type of information one gets through ESP.

Swann's procedure for leaving the body is very simple—probably since it is an inborn gift he possesses. He just decides where he wants to send his mind, visualizes the point, and then pushes his mind over to that location. Sometimes he will actually feel his mind traveling during the projection, although he will remain consciously alert.

Richard Greene has collected accounts from his students that also indicate that visualization exercises can successfully catalyze OBEs. Although admitting that some students take longer to develop the ability than others, Greene believes that his techniques will work for just about anyone, given sufficient time and practice. The accounts he has collected often read very similar to the accounts of those who have had OBEs spontaneously or through other methods. This is certainly qualitative evidence that his students are undergoing genuine OBEs. For instance, the following description was written by a student trying to transfer his consciousness into a lightbulb:

> At first, I had a hard time feeling myself in the position of the lightbulb. I would no sooner feel myself there when I would find myself being drawn back into my physical body. It was as if there was a great struggle to keep myself where I wanted to be. For a few moments in fact, I got the impression that I was bouncing back and forth between my body and the lightbulb. Once I got centered into the bulb, I could feel the closeness of the wall (there was a wall near to the bulb). At first I also found my mind analyzing and trying to remember the room as I usually knew it to be. What I was trying to do was to utilize my memory of the room. I also noticed that when I tried to analyze, remember, or intellectualize about what something should look like, I found myself back in the body. At one point I tried to see my own physical body from the bulb. As I looked at it, I noticed that I was looking down at my body, but I couldn't get a perception as to the color of my clothes, or the shape of my hair. In trying to intellectualize (or remember, if you will) how these things looked, I found myself immediately back in the body. This sort of thing occurred about three or four times and I naturally thought that I was simply imagining or visualizing what I was "seeing." Suddenly there came an incident which I found to be of great interest. Below the lightbulb were two boxes. I did not know what was in them. From my position, as the lightbulb, I could look

down into them. What I saw was that one box had some sort of cord or wire in it. The other box had scraps of paper in it. The word "seeing" to describe the way I saw these things is not the right word. They were images which penetrated into my consciousness. Along with the perceptions came a solid feeling of them being totally and completely right. If you close your eyes and visualize a red triangle—the way it appears in the mind's eye is the way I saw these things. I then returned my consciousness back to my body and went to look into the boxes. In one box there was wire which I found out later went to a guitar amplifier, and in the other there were pieces of paper. One other thing was that as I was the lightbulb, I noticed that the position of the boxes in regards to the lamp was not directly over the boxes, but rather to one side of them. When I got up to check my results, I saw that the bulb was in one direction away from the box rather than directly over them. And I also noticed that when I had looked at the boxes from the bulb's perspective, I had actually been the lamp. For in checking out what I saw through my fusing with the bulb, by going over physically to the bulb and looking from its perspective, I saw exactly the same thing as when I was fused consciously with the light bulb.

As for actual mental traveling, compare the following report to the typical OBE narrative:

I projected my consciousness out of my physical body to a friend that I had not spoken to in about three weeks. I was familiar with the person's apartment and what it looks like. I could feel myself there almost immediately. I was outside the apartment door at first. I then tried to walk through the door, but I found that I had a hard time entering and could not pass through it. I turned around so that I would be entering the door backwards. I found that it was very easy then to enter through the door. Once through, I turned around and proceeded to locate my friend. I saw that she was in the kitchen in the rear of the apartment. I saw her drinking coffee and watching television. I also got the impression that she had a typewriter in front of her and I got the impression that she may have been typing. I then tried to get her to see or feel me. To do this I tried touching her shoulder, but she did not seem

*to respond. I stayed at her apartment for a while longer and
then finally returned to my physical body. After I returned I
called her long distance and asked her about the things that I
had seen.*

*At the time I had traveled to her, she had been drinking coffee
and watching television. She said the typewriter was NOT on
the table in front of her and that she had not been typing at
all. However, she said that at about the time that I had been
there, she had been thinking of typing a letter to a friend of
hers somewhere in Chicago. So the thought of typing was in
her conscious mind. As to her feeling me, she said that she had
received no particular feelings such as a touch, but that at
about that time she had suddenly had a flash of me in her
mind and she started thinking about me for a while.*

Note here how mind traveling, or traveling clairvoyance, can entail a mixture of (apparent) genuine observation with what appears to be ESP-
gathered information. This paradox has led some parapsychologists to
argue that the OBE is merely a subjective altered state of consciousness
during which one can make use of the mind's innate extrasensory powers.
It is also possible, however, that the mind may be very open to ESP
impressions after becoming independent of the body and its brain. The
mind might automatically process these impressions as it is making its
observations. Some natural confusion might result.

The fact that visualization can help induce a limited form of OBE is
also exemplified by a phenomenon callled remote viewing—a modern-day
version of the traveling clairvoyance so well known during the age of the
great mesmerists. The basic procedures, first developed by Ingo Swann as
an adjunct to his OBE gifts, were later formalized by researchers at the
Stanford Research Institute (now S.R.I. International) in Menlo Park,
California, when they realized that this technique could be learned by
other psychics and even lay people. Remote viewing has become one of
parapsychology's most popular instruments for helping people learn and
display ESP—and is also inherently linked to the OBE.

The remote viewing work all began when Swann, whose powers were
being tested at S.R.I. at the time, told two physicists there that he could
send his mind anywhere in the world. All he needed was a set of latitude
and longitude lines, and he could project there, see what the terrain was

like, and report back. Russell Targ and Harold Puthoff were astounded by this claim and decided to test him on the spot. They were right in the middle of an ESP test at the time, but Swann was bored, and they wanted to humor him. So they called out some coordinates and waited to see what their subject would report. The results of the impromptu experiment were so stunning that Targ and Puthoff began focusing on this curious phenomenon. Over the next several weeks, they challenged Swann continually with remote viewing tasks. They would merely choose the coordinates. Swann would sit back in an easy chair at the testing offices, project his mind to the proper location, and tell everyone what he saw. His accuracy was amazing.

Sometimes there were surprises. For one experiment, the physicists gave Swann coordinates for what they thought would be the middle of Lake Victoria in Africa. Swann sent his mind to the locale and described flying over a large body of water and coming to rest on a piece of land nearby. This did not make sense to Targ and Puthoff, who hurried to recheck their atlas. They discovered that those specific coordinates pinpointed a peninsula jutting out into the lake!

Swann eventually participated in nearly 100 of these remote viewing sessions. He was successful 75 times, missed on 14 occasions, and six others could not be evaluated. Targ and Puthoff also ran a series of tests in which one of them would drive to a randomly chosen site in the San Francisco Bay area. Swann, who had no idea where the experimenter had driven, was asked to project himself to the outbound experimenter and report what he saw. His descriptions were often correct and detailed. He could describe where the experimenter was, the terrain, nearby buildings, and even the landscape.

The procedure Swann uses for his remote viewing is a form of OBE travel, although he often seems reticent about admitting it. I was able to interview Swann when he visited Los Angeles in 1976 as part of a promotional tour for a book he had written. I was curious to know whether Swann really felt that he was leaving the body during his remote viewing trials or merely using ESP to gain visual impressions about the distant areas. "Remote viewing is not much different from daydreaming," he explained. "At the time you're supposed to contact the outbound experimenter, you just agree with yourself that you're going to do it. You sort of think about him and you'll start to get a flood of images starting to come in."

This certainly did not strike me as true mind-traveling. I raised this issue with Swann, who then admitted that different subjects may use different strategies for accomplishing remote viewing, including actual mind projection. "Some people," he said alluding to himself, "often report a sense of moving to the place. They report going over streams of water or desert. They get to the places and often comment on things they would comment on when getting off an airplane—the humidity, the wind, or the cold, and so on." Swann sometimes experiences just this type of traveling during his own remote viewing attempts. The psychic ended our discussion by admitting that remote viewing could be done either way, from within the body or from without.

Swann should know, since he has helped other psychics develop remote viewing skills. The most successful was the late Pat Price, an ex-Burbank, California, police official who was tested at S.R.I. on several occasions. Targ and Puthoff instituted a formalized experimental plan during their work with this rather unlikely psychic superstar. They first selected a pool of geographical locations in and about the Bay area. One experimenter would secretly drive to a randomly selected site and remain there for several minutes, while the other experimenter remained at S.R.I. with Price. After the outbound experimenter had arrived at the designated location, the other researcher would ask Price to make psychic contact, mentally visit his location, and report what he saw. Price would use a procedure similar to Swann's to accomplish the task. He would sit back, relax, free his mind, and give himself the suggestion to go to the outbound experimenter and see where he was. Sometimes he would also sketch what his mind saw. About six sessions constituted a formal series. Transcripts were typed from Price's reports and given in random order to an outside judge. The judge then visited the various locations and tried to guess which transcript was meant for which location.

The results were phenomenal! Not only could Price describe the target areas in detail, he could even name the building or site where the outbound experimenter was situated. The judge usually had no trouble making the matchups.

The next step in the S.R.I. remote viewing work came when other people were tested with the procedure, including various staff members and even one or two resident skeptics. The researchers were surprised to find that remote viewing capabilities appear to be quite common. Many people who did not ordinarily consider themselves psychic were very successful when they put their minds to it.

The remote viewing procedure has now also been replicated by other researchers: at Mundelein College in Chicago, at the Institute for Parapsychology in Durham, at the Lawrence-Berkeley Laboratories in northern California, and at other prestigious laboratories. It is one of the most popular testing procedures in use today.

Although remote viewing does not necessarily entail an OBE, it does teach people to visualize. In fact, remote viewing may be considered a visualization technique useful for inducing the OBE. Many remote viewers eventually began traveling to the target areas, as if they were learning to leave the body through the art of the visualization process.

Targ and Puthoff have even gathered some tentative data to support the view that some remote viewing entails a mind/body separation. Some of their best subjects have been able to "fly over" to the target areas and report buildings and aspects of the terrain not visible to the outbound experimenters. The S.R.I. team eventually hopes to document the mind-separation component of the remote viewing experience by setting up delicate oscillators and other equipment at the target sites. They plan to see if a mind viewing the location can influence the equipment readings and functionings. This would indicate that the subject's mind may be actually "present" there in some respect.

Most parapsychologists see remote viewing as an end in itself, a rather simple procedure for testing people's ESP that often seems to work somewhat reliably. Few appreciate the fact that remote viewing may be the first step to developing out-of-body skills and may be as valid a training procedure as the exercises listed in the previous section. Merely visualizing a distant location could be the first step in experiencing mind travel.

If you wish to learn remote viewing yourself, it is easy enough to do. Proceed slowly at first.

For your first pilot attempts, have a friend photograph several areas in your hometown. Choose one, look at it, and then sit back in a comfortable chair in your room or home and visualize it. Hold the image in your mind for as long as you can. Imagine yourself leaving the body, traveling to the area, and floating about it. Take a look at the area in as much detail as possible. It might be a good idea to report what you are seeing and experiencing into a tape recorder.

Now compare what you have seen with the photograph. Especially note anything you saw that does not appear in the photograph. It may be some landscaping behind a building, another structure to the side of it, or anything else. Make a special note of these extra details and then drive to the location. See if any of your extraneous observations are correct. If they are, and you have never visited the site before, your remote viewing has been successful.

You should practice this visualization procedure weekly until definite paranormal information starts cropping up in your reports. Then you will be ready for the next phase in your development.

Again you will have to recruit a friend. Ask him or her to choose about two dozen areas around town—all as different as possible so that eventual identification will be easy. For one day each week have your friend pick one of these locations at random and drive there while you remain home. Sit back and wait until you are sure the person has arrived at the target location; then visualize yourself traveling to find him or her. Give yourself the mental suggestion that your mind will be drawn to your friend's whereabouts like a magnet. It should not take long before you actually "see" where he or she is located. Report into a tape recorder everything you see, including the geography, any buildings in the area, and what your friend is doing there. Later, type up your narrative. Run this experiment six times. Then give your friend all six of the transcripts in random order, and see if he or she can correctly match them as to places.

At first you will probably not induce a full-fledged OBE. But as you continue to practice and give yourself suggestions that your mind is leaving the body during the procedure, you might find yourself really traveling while you remote-view. As the wise occultists remind their students, worry only about mastering the procedures. You will have your OBE when the mind is ready for it.

There does seem to be an art or skill to successful remote viewing. Alan Vaughan, a researcher and psychic now living in Los Angeles, suggests that you keep the following points in mind (which I have slightly revised) while practicing:

1. *Report what you see, not what you "think." Report all the images that flash through your mind. Do not censor anything.*

2. *Draw what you see if you think you can.*

3. *Do not try to make sense out of the images that come to mind. Just take them as they come, and do not attempt to be analytical.*

4. *You may want to focus on the shapes, forms, and colors of the objects or buildings you see.*

5. *Do not become confused if something you see doesn't make sense. Report it anyway.*

6. *Visit the target sites after you have completed your session or series. Pay close attention to details of the area you saw but that your friend did not or could not have seen.*

7. *Do not do too many sessions in a short space of time.*

In short, remote viewing can be an end in itself or virtually a training procedure for the development of OBE skills. Many remote viewing subjects experience this phenomenon even without any training in formal OBE induction techniques. Good luck!

There is one practical problem with the use of visualization, however, that few writers on the subject ever discuss. Unfortunately, not everyone has keen powers of visualization. Many people are capable of rather intense mental imagery and can become absorbed in their mental creations. But very poor visualizers have a difficult time holding or retaining even the simplest images. If you happen to be a poor visualizer, the exercises outlined in this chapter may not be suitable for you. There are books on the market that outline exercises for developing and improving imagery skills. But a person's ability to develop visualization skills seems to be a deeply ingrained part of his or her individual psychology. Some people just cannot develop imagery abilities. I know a psychologist who is so bad at visualization that she cannot even visualize her home and tell you how many windows it contains. She literally has to sit down and calculate it out by counting exterior and common walls! You might wish to test your own imagery potentials before trying to produce an OBE through this method.

This does not mean that you have to possess strong imagery abilities in order to have an OBE. Dr. Harvey Irwin, a psychologist at the University of New England in Armindale, Australia, has found that people who have had spontaneous OBEs do not differ very much in their imagery capabilities from what is normal for an average adult. But the use of visualization to *develop* OBE skills may not be the best bet for those of you who have trouble with mental imagery.

How do you know whether you are a natural imager or not? Several complicated psychological tests would let you know. But an obvious method is through practice. Just test yourself. Visualize your home and see if you can count how many windows it contains. If you have trouble with this simple task, you might not be the type of person who normally thinks in visual images. Another very simple, rough way to see if you can really become absorbed in your mental imagery is to take the test outlined below. This survey has been extracted and adapted from a complicated test that gauges many aspects of an individual's cognitive style. Mark each question true or false as it pertains to you individually.

> *1. I can be greatly moved by eloquent or poetic language.*
>
> *2. While watching a movie, a television show, or a play, I may become so involved that I forget about myself and my surroundings and experience the story as if it were real and as if I were taking part in it.*
>
> *3. Sometimes I feel as if my mind could envelop the whole world.*
>
> *4. I can imagine (or daydream) some things so vividly that they hold my attention as a good movie or story does.*
>
> *5. It is sometimes possible for me to be completely immersed in nature or in art and to feel as if my whole state of consciousness has somehow been temporarily altered.*

If you have marked more items false than true, perhaps the procedures outlined in the earlier chapters will be more useful for you.

Even if many of you do not find yourselves leaving the body as a result of these exercises, you will benefit from practicing them. The inner world of mental imagery is fascinating and is quickly becoming one of psychology's most provocative new frontiers. The world of mental experience is far more entertaining and self-revealing than the often dull messages we receive from the physical world. So, if you cannot leave the body through the use of mental images, at least use them to go within yourself. You may learn just as much.

REFERENCES

Blackmore, Susan. *Parapsychology and Out-of-the-Body Experiences.* East Sussex, England: Transpersonal Books, 1978.

————. Have you ever had an OBE?: The wording of the question. *Journal of the Society for Psychical Research,* 1982, *51,* 292-302.

Greene, Richard. *The Handbook of Astral Projection.* Cambridge, Mass: Next Step Publications, 1979.

Irwin, Harvey. Out of the body down under: Some cognitive characteristics of Australian students reporting OBEs. *Journal of the Society for Psychical Research,* 1980, *50,* 448-59.

King, Francis. *Astral Projection, Magic and Alchemy.* London: Neville Spearman, 1971.

Richards, Steve. *Levitation.* Wellingborough, England: Aquarian Press, 1980.

Samuels, Mike, and Samuels, Nancy. *Seeing with the Mind's Eye.* New York: Harper & Row, 1975.

Scholem, G. *Jewish Mysticism.* New York: Schocken, 1961.

Swann, Ingo. *To Kiss Earth Good-bye.* New York: Hawthorn, 1975.

Targ, Russell and Puthoff, Harold. *Mind-Reach.* New York: Delacorte Press, 1977.

Vaughan, Alan. Remote viewing—ESP for everyone. *Psychic,* 1976, *7,* 32-35.

Walker, Benjamin. *Beyond the Body.* London: Routledge & Kegan Paul, 1974.

chapter eight
Projection Through Dream Control

A special age-old relationship exists between sleep and the out-of-body experience. Many primitive cultures believe that the soul wanders away from the body during sleep, and for this reason, a sleeper is never moved from where he or she is located. There may be more fact than fable to this myth, since most people have their first spontaneous OBEs while either falling asleep or emerging from sleep. Many talented projectors, from Hugh Callaway to Sylvan Muldoon to Keith Harary, experienced nocturnal separations before learning voluntary control over them. Many techniques for inducing the OBE, such as those outlined by Robert Monroe, teach the student to bring him- or herself to the point of sleep. Therefore, it makes considerable sense that the OBE might be most easily induced from this state of unconsciousness. But how? How can the unconscious sleeper "do" anything to voluntarily leave the body? The answer comes through dream control.

BACKGROUND

Few people realize that dreams can be controlled very easily. You have probably noted that your dreams are often influenced by what you do during the day, the people you meet, your interactions with them, and how you feel about your friends and relatives. Our relationship with people meaningful in our lives often dictate, on a symbolic level, what we dream each night. Yet, it is just as possible to control the content of your dreams through auto-suggestion. If you go to sleep deliberately concentrating on a certain person and theme, you will find in time that the unconscious mind will respond to the suggestions.

The ultimate form of dream control is producing "lucid" dreams in which you realize that you are dreaming but do not subsequently wake up. Many people have this experience once or twice in their lives. The most common form of lucidity occurs during a nightmare, when the dreamer realizes the experience is unreal and orders him- or herself to awaken. More proficient lucid dreamers are able to remain asleep after making this identification and can then go on to experiment with their dream environments. They can create all sorts of miracles barred from us in our real day-to-day lives. Flying about is a favorite adventure of the lucid dreamer. The important thing to remember is that, while some people are natural lucid dreamers, the ability can be developed and nurtured with practice.

People who become aware that they are dreaming have rather remarkable control over themselves; the conscious and unconscious minds literally seem to merge. A curious finding along these lines has been made by Keith Hearne of Hull University in England, who has discovered that lucid dreams can be artificially induced in laboratory volunteers. Special clips attached to the dreamer's nose are electrically charged when the subject has entered a REM (rapid eye movement) period, which denotes dreaming. Pulses sent through the clip alert the sleeper, who will "wake up" to the fact that he or she is dreaming. The sleeper can then signal back to the experimenter through a prearranged eye movement pattern that he or she is aware of the state. This research has now given investigators a method of directly interacting with the unconscious. The experimental induction of the lucid dream may well be one of psychology's greatest breakthroughs. Researchers in the field of creativity hope to train lucid dreamers to create adventures for themselves that can serve as the basis for later plays and stories, while psychotherapists hope that a lucid dreamer can train him- or herself to meet a dream "helper" who will aid the dreamer in understanding the problems in his or her life and possible solutions to them.

Parapsychologists are also keenly aware of the potential benefits that lucid dreaming might offer their own field. Many lucid dreamers report ESP experiences as part of their dreams, and some pilot work has been carried out to see if the lucid dreaming state of mind may be particularly conducive to ESP. A very special—and empirical—relationship also exists between lucid dreaming and the OBE.

Most of the great projectors of the past were also lucid dreamers. Many of them even learned the art of astral projection as a by-product of their experiments in dream control. Just why this curious relationship exists is not clear. There is good reason to believe that unconscious factors play an important role in the ability to leave the body; perhaps learning conscious control of one's unconscious mental processes is a critical factor in the ability to produce OBEs at will. This theory is supported by the fact that people who try to induce lucid dreaming sometimes also produce OBEs quite accidentally.

As mentioned earlier, Sylvan Muldoon, Hugh Callaway, and many others claimed that at least some of their OBEs were induced through the manipulation of lucid dreaming. The basic skill was to achieve a lucid or preprogrammed dream, direct themselves to leave the body, and then "awake" outside of it. Such a practice led Callaway to realize that the lucid dream could be used as a road to purely volitional control of the OBE.

Lucid dreaming and the OBE represent forms of mental life divorced from the body. Although some lucid dreams may actually be disguised OBEs, these two phenomena seem to be discrete mental experiences. The lucid dreamer is quite aware that he or she is dreaming and that the experience is imaginary. His or her awareness is dreamlike, sometimes fantastic. The astral projector mentally functions in a more concrete environment and is usually aware that he or she is definitely *not* dreaming. So it would be naive to claim that OBEs induced through lucid dreaming are merely dreams themselves. The best way to view the lucid dream, then, is as a steppingstone to the OBE and not merely as a parallel phenomenon existing side by side to it. As one attempts to control the unconscious mind during sleep and quasi-sleep (that is, the hypnagogic state), lucid dreaming might be the first manifestation of this control. OBEs may follow naturally. Learning to induce lucid dreams may well represent a very practical way of igniting spontaneous OBEs, from which more formal and directional control may be established.

The ability to lucid dream is not a mystical gift—a strange phenomenon, yes, but not a paranormal one. Since it is a potential that is open to all of us, it represents a perfect means of approaching the OBE.

THE TECHNIQUES

Before learning to induce lucid dreaming, you must learn to observe and control your dreams in general. The key is simple auto-suggestion coupled with systematic observation. An excellent discussion on dream control comes from Patricia Garfield, a San Francisco psychologist who is herself a lucid dreamer, in her book *Creative Dreaming*, which may be consulted for more elaborate discussion and suggestions. Here we are concerned just with the basics.

After studying several systems of dream control and use taught in various independent cultures, Dr. Garfield suggests certain steps for learning formal dream control.

Begin by re-evaluating your attitudes toward your dreams. You must convince yourself, either through self-observation or academic study, that your dreams are important and meaningful to you and that you can learn from them. If you recall a dream upon waking, don't ignore it. Try to analyze it and see what messages it holds for you.* Once you have realized the importance of your dreams, you can begin to experiment with influencing them. If you respect your dreams, they will respond.

The basic technique is to give yourself suggestions before you go to sleep that you will subsequently dream about a certain person and subject. If you practice regularly, you will note your suggestions being incorporated into your reveries. Garfield specifically suggests that "you may wish to put your dream intention into a phrase, relax, repeat it, and visualize its fulfillment." A phrase such as "tonight I will dream about my friend so-and-so" will suffice. When you get into bed, in other words, don't just drift off to sleep. Prepare yourself for your dreams.

By using this psychological exercise, you will also find that your dream recall improves. This will occur more and more frequently as you begin gaining some control of your dream content. It will also help if you write down your dreams in the morning. The best way is to lie still when

---

*For an excellent guide on this subject, see Montague Ullman (with Nan Zimmerman), <u>Working with Dreams</u> (New York: Delacorte, 1979).

you wake; just rest there and try to remember what you have been dreaming. If you can't remember, change position. For some reason this occasionally ignites dream recall. Then, as soon as the dream comes to mind, write it out or recite it into a tape recorder. This way you will have a record of your dreams and will be able to see how your control of them is advancing. You might find that dream memories will start coming back spontaneously during the day, usually sparked by something you see or hear that is similar to what you dreamed the night before.

Once you have achieved some level of dream control, you can proceed to induce lucid dreams. There are many ways this can be done; the simplest is through one or another form of self-suggestion. Be advised, however, that lucid dreams are most prone to occur in the morning hours after you have had a good night's sleep. So your best bet is to practice after you initially awake, but plan to go back to sleep for awhile. This phenomenon may be the outcome of the normal psychology of sleep, since most people do not begin their night's first dream period until 70-90 minutes after dozing off. We usually wake up from a REM (rapid eye movement) state, so returning to sleep may put you right back into one. Your suggestion to lucid dream at this critical time may be more easily acted on than during initial sleep onset.

The following are basic techniques for inducing lucid dreams:

1. *Induce flying dreams. For some reason, lucid dreamers almost universally experience more flying dreams than does the average dreamer. People who have many lucid dreams often find that they are heralded by flying dreams or that lucidity can best be achieved during the flying dream. It may simply be that the gravitation-defying content of such a dream alerts the dreamer to the fact that he or she is dreaming. Therefore, begin by giving yourself the suggestion that you will fly in your dreams. When you have succeeded, lucid dreams may begin manifesting spontaneously.*

2. *Induce stress or nightmares. Almost everyone has had the experience of making him- or herself awake from a particularly ferocious nightmare. This psychological defense against too much stress in dreams can be put to genuine advantage. Suggest to yourself that you will have a nightmare or an especially stressful adventure in your dreams, and see if you can awake yourself from it. Give yourself the suggestion that you will wake up when the dream becomes so stressful that you realize you are dreaming. After you have accomplished this*

goal, do not order yourself to wake after you become lucid. Merely will your dream environment to change or tell whoever or whatever is threatening you to go away! They—or it!— usually will. Some cultures even teach children to control their nightmares in this way, by reminding themselves when they go to sleep that dreams are unreal and to make friends with their dream enemies by using this very form of confrontation.

3. *Recognize incongruities in your dreams. This is probably the most universal method for learning and controlling lucid dreaming. Before you go to sleep, give yourself the suggestion that during your dreams, you will be able to think analytically. Tell yourself to note any incongruities that will alert you to the unreality of what you are experiencing.*

Most people have their first lucid dreams when, for some inexplicable reason, this moment of insight occurs spontaneously. For example, one of my own lucid dreams occurred one morning after I had gotten up, read a little on lucid dreaming, and dozed off on the couch. I dreamed that I was in a pool hall with a young lady. We left the building and, as I turned around, the girl disappeared in a flash. This puzzled me, so I went back into the pool hall, only to find that it had been completely redecorated. From this incongruity, I realized that I was dreaming. I did not awake, but I gave myself the suggestion to remain asleep so that I could experiment with my dream environment. I had the time of my life flying about and deliberately trying to achieve an expanded state of consciousness. Finally, I ordered myself to awaken.

To catch such incongruities, repeated self-suggestion is the best way to proceed, although it may take considerable time and practice.

4. *Suggest to yourself that dreams are unreal. To the dreamer, the dream world is very real. Who hasn't awakened from a nightmare in a cold sweat, or laughing at some absurdity? It is possible to change all this merely through suggestion. Mary Arnold-Forster, a British housewife who is an accomplished lucid dreamer, explains how she nurtured her ability in her book* Studies in Dreaming. *Throughout the day she began reminding herself that dreams are not real. This acted as an auto-suggestion on her unconscious mind and she started to remember while she was dreaming. Lucid dreaming was the natural result. Usually she awoke as soon as she realized she was dreaming,*

but in time she was able to catch herself from getting too excited, allowing the dream to run its course.

5. *Hold awareness up to the moment of sleep onset and suggest that you will observe your dreams with conscious awareness. The deliberate induction of the lucid dream from the waking state, rather than from within a dream itself, is probably the most difficult technique, first outlined by the Russian mystic P.D. Ouspensky in his classic study,* A New Model of the Universe. *The procedure was an outgrowth of his fascination with the hypnagogic state. To observe this state in as much detail as possible, Ouspensky practiced holding on to awareness up to the point when he actually fell asleep. Gradually, he learned that he could maintain consciousness even after he had dozed off, which allowed him to observe his dreams with the full realization that they* were *dreams. His method of inducing lucid dreams was, therefore, to observe the hypnagogic state, prolong it, and then consciously guide himself into sleep. During this process he held a thought or idea rigidly in his mind, willing it to appear in his subsequent dream.*

In reading Ouspensky's writings, however, it is really not clear if his lucid dreams were genuine, or just very complicated successions of hypnagogic imagery. Since no clear psychophysiological differentiation exists between the state immediately preceding slumber and the first stages of sleep, perhaps the point is academic—especially since the hypnagogic state is ideal for inducing OBEs, as we shall see shortly.

As already pointed out, inducing lucid dreams may well prompt the spontaneous manifestation of OBEs. If you wish *deliberately* to induce OBEs from the lucid dream, however, following are three of the most commonly employed techniques:

1. *When you have achieved a lucid dream, order yourself to return to the confines of your body, but remind yourself not to wake up. At this point you will usually find yourself back in the body. You will be either cataleptic or, to your amazement, you will be able to see your room clearly even though you are aware that your eyes are closed. This is because, even though you are actually still asleep, you may* think *you are awake. Now merely order yourself to leave the body by floating away from it. An OBE will usually result.*

2. *A somewhat different method has been suggested by J.H.M. White-man, a mathematician from Capetown, South Africa, who is also a*

habitual projector. He explains in his autobiography that a lucid dream can be turned into an OBE merely by an exercise of mind. When you find yourself in a lucid dream, try to clear the mind. Block out your dream environment and observe the very process of your own thought. Your dream milieu will collapse, and you may find yourself out-of-body.

3. *A third suggestion comes from Sylvan Muldoon, who believed that flying dreams automatically signify that the dreamer [i.e., his "astral" body] is unconsciously out-of-body, although the mind may still be locked in the physical body. Muldoon suggests that a lucid dream of flying be induced, or you should begin to fly in your dream, and then order yourself to awake out-of-body. This was a favorite method he used for nocturnal projections.*

The strange relationship between dreaming, sleeping, and out-of-body travel plays an important role in Muldoon's writings. He even developed a method of projection through control of dreaming and/or the hypnagogic state, which resembled that of P.D. Ouspensky:

For several nights after you retire (several weeks would be better) watch yourself during the process of going to sleep. Try to concentrate your thoughts within yourself. Think of nothing and no one but yourself. Try to keep a close watch upon yourself, as your consciousness grows dim. Try to remember that you are awake, but still going to sleep. You will catch the significance of this when you try it—far more than you do now, while reading it.

After you have learned to hold consciousness well up into the hypnagogic state, until you actually are enveloped in sleep, then you must go a step further and construct a proper dream to hold in mind, while going to sleep. Remember: the dream must be constructed so that you are going to be active in it; and further, it must be constructed so that the action you go through will correspond to the route taken by the phantom when projected.

What do you like to do? Swim? Ride in an aeroplane? Go up in a balloon? A ferris wheel? An elevator? Be sure and do (in your dream) the thing you "like" to do. If you select something you do not like, the sensation will interiorize you, for it will be unpleasant. Do that which will give you a sensation which you like, and if you become fully conscious, once you are projected, you will like the sensation which you will actually get from the phantom floating in the air. This will go a long way toward ultimate success—to have the action in the dream of such a nature that you enjoy the sensation.

Now let us suppose that you enjoy going up in an elevator. (This is the formula I use.) You have already learned to hold consciousness up to the time you go to sleep. Lie upon your back. Think within yourself. You are lying upon your back on the floor of an elevator. You are going to lie there quietly and go to sleep, and as you enter sleep the elevator is going to move upward. And you are going to enjoy the sensation of going up, as you lie upon your back on the floor of the elevator.

Now it is trembling a little, getting ready to go up to the top story of a large building. Slowly, quietly, it is going up, going up, going up! You are conscious that you are moving upward. You are enjoying the sensation to the utmost. It is nearing the top story now. It has stopped. You are going to rise to your feet and walk out of the elevator and round the floor of the upper story of the building.

You are going to look all about you, as you walk round, observing everything. Now you are going to walk back into the elevator and lie down upon your back on the floor. Slowly you are moving downward, slowly downward, and now you are lying on your back on the floor of the elevator, on the ground floor of the building.

I have stated that this was the dream I constructed for the purpose of inducing the astral body to emerge from the physical. Now, it is important to use the same dream over and over again; for if you try first one dream and then another, the subconscious will not be impressed with the construction (of the dream) as strongly as if you repeat the same one over and over each night, as you are entering sleep.

Have the dream vividly worked out in your mind, and hold it before you as your consciousness is slowly diminishing; shift yourself right into the "elevator" just as the moment of "unknowingness" comes to you; and the astral body will move upward in the elevator; it will upright itself above the shell, just as you dream of standing up when the elevator reaches the top floor; it will move outward, just as you dream you are walking out of the elevator. Likewise, on the return, as you walk into the elevator, the astral will move to a position directly over the shell; as you lie down, the astral will resume the horizontal position; as the elevator lowers itself, the astral body will lower itself also.

After you have learned to induce and control your preprojection dream successfully, you are ready to use it to induce the actual separation.

Up to this point, it does not seem to matter whether or not the dream is lucid. To induce a full separation, however, you must remember to wake yourself from your dream after you have left the elevator. So, at some point, lucidity must be established in the dream. This should automatically induce the OBE state. You should find yourself hovering above your body.

Although Muldoon does not actually make the point outright, you should eventually try to make the whole dream lucid so that you can become actively involved in it. This will allow you to remind yourself to have an OBE at the appropriate time. The entire technique seems to represent a form of self-suggestion coupled with visualization.

All these exercises may sound hard to master, but they really are not. The only thing you have to do is practice them with the conviction that they will eventually work. It is all rather like biofeedback training. Psychologists have learned that we all possess a certain degree of control over what were once thought to be autonomic physiological functions—including brain waves, heart rate, electrical skin resistance, and body temperature. Most people can learn to control these functions merely by receiving feedback about them. One common method for brain-wave control, for example, is to hook a subject to an EEG linked to a bell system. When the subject momentarily produces a certain brain-wave rhythm, such as a sequence of alpha waves, the bell starts to ring. This feedback allows the subject to produce the desired results by trial and error. The subject usually begins by trying specific strategies, such as actively "willing" or creating certain mental pictures to produce the waves. Gradually, however, he or she will learn that a more passive approach is best. Biofeedback control is most successfully practiced merely by sitting back, relaxing, and passively "willing" the appropriate bodily changes to take place. This strategy, called "passive volition," works for most people no matter what biofeedback task they are given.

Translating this into more practical terms, it seems that learning to be *aware* of your mind/body functions gives you a degree of automatic control over them.

This also holds true for the exercises listed above. You will automatically develop some control over your dreams merely by observing them and giving yourself appropriate auto-suggestions. Your unconscious mind will do the rest. The reason most of us do not have any control over our dreams is because few of us really pay any attention to them. As Dr. Garfield wisely points out, the critical key to learning dream control is to develop the correct attitude toward your nocturnal creations. The rest is easy.

COMMENTS

To illustrate the usefulness of the exercises described above, let us see how the great projectors of the past used lucid dreaming as a route to the OBE. This will also reveal how the OBE often evolves in some sort of symbiotic relationship with this peculiar dream state.

The ability to lucid dream may automatically spark spontaneous OBEs; this is well illustrated in the reports of Dr. Frederick Van Eeden, a turn-of-the-century Dutch physician and psychologist who first described the phenomenon. Van Eeden began studying his own dreams in 1896 and kept detailed diaries on them. This observation process seems to have sparked his lucid dreaming, which began in 1897, and he eventually collected 352 accounts. Apparently he never attempted to induce lucid dreams, nor did he probably realize that he could do so. He first discovered the lucid dream when an incongruity alerted him to the state. "I dreamt that I was floating through a landscape with bare trees, knowing it was April," he explained in a lecture presented to the Society for Psychical Research many years later, " and I remarked that the perspective of the branches and twigs changed quite naturally. Then I made the reflection, during sleep, that my fancy would never be able to invent or to make an image as intricate as the perspective movement of little twigs seen in floating by." After realizing that he was only dreaming, he did not wake up so he was able to continue his observations.

This initial experience had an unusual side effect. Van Eeden started having OBEs, although the psychologist at first did not quite realize what was happening. For instance, six months after his first lucid dream, he had the following experience:

> In the night of January 19-20, I dreamt that I was lying in the garden before the windows of my study, and saw the eyes of my dog through the glass pane. I was lying on my chest and observing the dog very keenly. At the same time, however, I knew with perfect certainty that I was dreaming and lying on my back in my bed. And then I resolved to wake up slowly and carefully and observe how my sensation of lying on my chest would change into the sensation of lying on my back. And so I did, slowly and deliberately, and the transition—which I have since undergone many times—is most wonderful. It is like the feeling of slipping from one body into another, and there is distinctly a double recollection of the two bodies. I remembered what I felt in my dream lying on my chest; but returning into the day-life, I remembered also that my physical body had been quietly lying on its back all the while. This observation of a double memory I have had many times since. It is so indubitable that it leads almost unavoidably to the conception of a dream-body.

> ...In a lucid dream the sensation of having a body—having eyes, hands, a mouth that speaks, and so on—is perfectly distinct; yet I know at the same time that the physical body is sleeping and has quite a different position. In waking up, the sensations blend together, so to speak, and I remember as clearly the action of the dream-body as the restfulness of the physical body.

This experience led Van Eeden to wonder if his "dream body" might not be in some sense "real." He even suggested that this body and the "astral" body of the occultists were one and the same—indicating that he was partially aware that he was quite literally out-of-body. (Most lucid dreamers, although aware that they are dreaming, perceive their dream bodies as their real and only bodies. A dreamer who finds him- or herself out-of-body and aware that his or her physical body is located elsewhere is probably undergoing an OBE.)

After this adventure, Van Eeden began actively experimenting with the dream body and the lucid dream. Sometimes he would "awake" to find his dream body standing in his bedroom next to his wife. He even tried shouting at her to see if he could rouse her. These experiences were, of course, most likely genuine OBEs and not lucid dreams—of which he had plenty. His favorite pastime in his (genuine) lucid dreams was to fly about, meet with people he knew were dead, explore beautiful landscapes, and engage in other adventures. He also made some pertinent observations about the nature and phenomenology of the lucid dream. He noted that they always occurred in the morning between the hours of five and eight and usually manifested a day or two after he had experienced nonlucid flying dreams. Sometimes a lucid dream would lapse back into normal dreaming. He also described how he would occasionally "wake up" in his bedroom, only to see that the room was somehow unusual. Strange sights and sounds would manifest, thus alerting him that he was actually still asleep and dreaming! He would then have to reawaken himself.

Van Eeden's major contribution to the study of dreams was published by the Society for Psychical Research in 1913. A keen student of psychical research as well as dream psychology, Van Eeden hoped eventually to write a more complete history of his experiments. Apparently he never completed this work. Perhaps in this projected work he would have more clearly differentiated between his lucid dreams and his OBEs. In reading his paper today, however, it seems obvious that he was having both experiences, although he makes no differentiation between them. His records best serve as an illustration of how the OBE exists in close relationship to lucid dreaming and can be considered a by-product of it.

Patricia Garfield, whose research on dreams was discussed earlier, particularly recommends the use of lucid dreaming for enjoyment and psychological and spiritual growth. (Or, as she puts it, "a kind of learning that is not contained in psychology books.") She experienced a dramatic OBE during the time of her active experimentation. In her autobiographical *Pathway to Ecstasy*, Dr. Garfield describes how she was resting one day on her bed just ready to fall asleep. She had been reading a book on the OBE and decided to carry her experiments one step further. She noticed that her body was gently vibrating and she heard whirring sounds fluttering in her ears. Realizing that she might well be in a pre-OBE state, she willed herself to float away from her body. The suggestion worked and soon she found herself hovering over her own body. She lowered herself back down and then induced a second OBE. This time, however, her second self took off on its own, propelling itself away from the body at the speed of light. Garfield found herself in a void and then lost consciousness.

The experience had a strange, almost morbid effect on her, and she was frightened. All that day she felt as if she would have another OBE if she rested and let down her guard. Eventually she went to sleep on her side to inhibit any incipient OBE from manifesting.

Only much later did Dr. Garfield fully understand what had happened to her. "By assembling my own experience with lucid dreaming and comparing it with the recoded experiences of others," she writes in *Pathway to Ecstasy*, "I saw that I had been on an inevitable path to the out-of-the-body experience." She had learned that the techniques for inducing lucid dreaming are identical to ways of literally freeing one's self from the body. Learn one skill and you get a bonus!

Garfield has never been too comfortable with the prospect of leaving the body. When I first met her in San Francisco in 1979, she admitted that she had subsequently attempted conscious induction of the experience, but with little success. No doubt her initial negative reaction to the OBE reinforced her personal "fear barrier," which may have cut her off from any further exploration.

To understand the great complexities of the lucid dream and how it relates to conscious control of the OBE, however, one must turn to the detailed records of Hugh Callaway. He virtually mastered the art of conscious projection through his study of lucid dreaming.

We know relatively little about Callaway. Born in 1886, he spent most of his life in London and eventually became a lawyer. He served in the British armed forces for two years during World War I and later became very involved in London's occult underground, ultimately becoming a theosophist. Callaway began experimenting with the OBE when he was only 16, which no doubt accounts for his later interest in the occult. His first autobiographical accounts appeared in 1920 in the *Occult Review*; they were later expanded into a book written (as were his articles) under the pseudonym of Oliver Fox. This volume, *Astral Projection—a record of out-of-the-body experiences,* has become one of the classics in the field. Callaway lived to see the outbreak of World War II, and died in 1949.

Callaway's psychic history begins with his childhood, but not until 1902 did he have an experience that prompted his interest in lucid dreaming and astral projection. One night he was dreaming about entering his house when the odd configuration of the curb stones caught his attention. They had rearranged themselves from their normal position. The startled teenager suddenly realized that he was dreaming. This revelation produced such a marked alteration in his level of consciousness that he lost control of the dream. He awoke awed and excited. The experience also led young Callaway to wonder if he could train himself to become aware during his dreams and prolong the lucidity.

Eventually he discovered an appropriate technique. "Before going to sleep I must impress upon my mind the desirability of not allowing the critical faculty to slumber," he writes in his autobiography. "It must be kept awake, ready to pounce on any inconsistency in the dream and recognize it as such." It took hundreds of experiments before Callaway succeeded in inducing lucid dreams, but it was not long before he started having OBEs as well. These projections, which Callaway at first considered mere variations of the lucid dream, began manifesting when he tried to prolong his dreams. He would be exploring some strange dream environment when he would gradually become aware of the "pull" of his physical body. His dream environment would fade away and he would find himself standing by his bed at home.

Over the next three years, Callaway systematically experimented with his lucid dreams, and this led him to make several discoveries about the relationship between the lucid dream and the OBE. The first was his discovery of the "false awakening," which Van Eeden was to discover and describe a few years later. Callaway learned that sometimes he would "awake" after a lucid dream only to find himself still asleep. He would recognize this state when he found himself clearly viewing his room while simultaneously aware that his eyes were closed. It did not take him long to realize that merely by an act of will, he could induce an OBE from the false awakening. His next discovery was that he would sometimes awaken from a lucid dream totally cataleptic—again, a preprojection state that could be easily utilized for leaving the body at will.

However, even up to 1905, Callaway was not sure where the lucid dream ended and the actual projection of the astral body began. His interest in finding out came later that year as a result of what seemed an idle boast. Callaway had been courting a young woman named Elsie, who lived across town. One day he was bragging to her about his projections when she, in a brilliant display of one-upmanship, began claiming the same ability. She even boasted that she would visit him that very night—and made good her promise, too! Callaway was understandably shocked when Elsie's apparition appeared in his bedroom just as he was about to fall asleep. He visited her the next day to report on the visitation, but before he could tell her what had happened, the young woman offered a detailed description of his room—correct in just about every respect!

This incident encouraged Callaway to experiment further with astral projection. Now determined to discover the parameters of the OBE as a phenomenon independent of lucid dreaming, he wanted to find a way to leave the body without falling asleep so that dreaming of any sort would not interfere.

The first critical experiment was made in July of 1908 when Callaway discovered that he could willfully induce preprojection catalepsy. (He called this the "trance condition.") His technique was to lie down, close his eyes, breathe rhythmically until he became drowsy, but retain conscious awareness until he could see his room through his closed eyelids. Then he merely had to will himself to leave the body. Once out of his physical prison, Callaway could project to anywhere he liked just by willing himself to travel. Sometimes he was literally catapulted out of his body, or he would be borne away as though by a great wind. Later he learned that he could induce the preprojection trance by lying down and forcibly squinting his eyes upward until paralysis overtook him. Then he would visualize a doorway at the top of his head and imagine himself rushing through it until he "popped" out of his body. The experience was often very unpleasant and later Callaway dropped the method.*

Callaway devoted the rest of his experiments, from 1907 to at least 1937, to exploring the nature of the OBE world. Many of his strange

---

*This technique, called the "pineal door" method, is recommended in many psychic development books and is taken directly from Callaway's writings. Few writers who suggest this method seem aware that Callaway specifically warned that this technique is very unpleasant and can have negative repercussions on the body.

adventures are reported in chronological order in his book. He experimented with visiting earthly locations, traveling over great distances in a flash, and even succeeded in visiting new dimensions of reality where he freely interacted with the residents. His fascination with the occult grew during these years, and his eventual goal was to use his OBEs to locate an incorporeal spiritual master who could help him along the road to spiritual perfection. One can only wonder whether he succeeded.

Callaway's records are particularly fascinating since they show how fully controlled OBE skills can be developed through the use of lucid dreaming. There is no evidence that Callaway was a natural projector. His initial separations manifested as a by-product of his experiments in dream control, and there is no reason to believe that he was unique in his ability to master astral projection in this manner. He was wise enough, however, to see the potential of his experiences, which allowed him to use his lucid dreams as a springboard for further psychic development. His autobiographical notes can, therefore, serve as a model for any student who wishes to use lucid dreaming as a step toward the OBE. They show how to proceed, what phenomenology to expect, how to use what one has learned for more conscious control, and so forth. But, remember that it took Callaway some five years to learn the art. That is not really too long; roughly equivalent to the time it takes to become reasonably proficient at playing a musical instrument.

Although the student may wish to use Callaway's methods as a guide in his or her own practice, it is not necessary to learn total control of lucid dreaming to induce the OBE. Brief moments of lucidity can work equally as well in igniting your initial experiences. In this respect, there is much to say for the Muldoon dream-control method. In fact, it was though a technique very similar to his that I learned to induce some of my own OBEs.

As explained in Chapter 4, my first separations were apparently catalyzed by my dietary plan and my desire for the experience. Between 1965 and 1967, these projections were fairly common, and gradually I learned to exert some control over them through a rough form of lucid dreaming.

One result of my initial OBEs was that for the first time in my life, I suddenly became very aware of my hypnagogic state. I had never before paid any attention to this presleep imagery phase, but now I found myself immersed in it. Each night as I dropped off to sleep, I would see a panorama of scenes before my eyes—sometimes brief, sometimes so elaborate that it seemed as if I were actually dreaming. The more attention I paid to these images, the more I developed the capacity to prolong the hypnagogic state. One night I was lying in bed very near sleep, well into the hypnagogic state and immersed in a "half-dream" in which I was driving wildly down a freeway. I was quite aware that I was dreaming, but the experience was very realistic and I fought to keep control of the car. Then it dawned on me that nothing would happen if I crashed. At that moment I had an intuitive feeling that if I crashed the car, I would leave the body. I deliberately swerved off the road and began to plunge down an embankment. I felt an instant and wonderful sense of relief as I found myself floating above my body.

Over the next few months I had several of these driving "dreams" and hypnagogic reveries. I could usually leave the body by manipulating them. My theory is that these very special dreams were messages produced by my unconscious when I had entered a preprojection state. Crashing the car was a method of *releasing control of my consciousness* so that the OBE could manifest. I did not ever experiment with trying to induce this particular imagery, however. The driving dreams always manifested spontaneously.

As another curious by-product of my new awareness, I began noticing certain symbols in my dreams which seemed to be alerting me to ways of getting out of the body. I did not exactly experience these clues as lucid dreams, but would merely get a flash of insight during a normal dream of a way to experience an OBE. This type of insight usually came when I was dreaming about a small chute or hole that I could hurl myself through! One of my most amusing encounters came during a dream in which I was walking down the corridor of a building. A large trash chute was in the wall next to me, and even though the dream did not actually become lucid, some instinct told me to jump into the chute. I awoke totally cataleptic and in a preprojection state. After a brief struggle, I was able to induce a brief OBE during which I hovered joyfully over my body.

These various experiences resulted from the spontaneous manifestation of imagery strategies of the sort Muldoon suggested for the conscious projection of nocturnal separations. It is, therefore, likely that one can learn to leave the body by the use of specially prepared dreams or hypnagogic strategies. The problem is how to discover just *which* symbols or dream scenarios will work best. Muldoon himself realized that the precise scenarios will differ from person to person. My own opinion is that *any* technique or preprepared dream sequence will work, as long as you give yourself the suggestion that it *will* work and fully expect it to.

The lesson here is that once you have initially left the body or are merely practicing, *your mind will start presenting you with clues and hints on how to best get out of your body.* During the time of my active experiments with out-of-body travel, I played very little with dream-induction methods. Yet as soon as I had opened the door, the experience triggered many changes in my dream and presleep life. This new awareness clued me as to new possibilities and potentials.

The final question is obvious. How do you know when an OBE produced through dream control *is* an OBE and not just a dream?

Most experienced practitioners can tell the difference experientially. To them, the subjective experience between being out-of-the-body and merely having a lucid dream is as clear as the difference between waking and dreaming for the average person. S. Keith Harary likes to explain that his OBEs differ in quality from his dreams as vividly as do his dreams from his waking life. There is no reason to doubt the core validity of this type of subjective assessment. At first, however, novice out-of-body travelers may have a hard time distinguishing an OBE from a lucid dream. Both Hugh Callaway and Frederick Van Eeden originally confused the two experiences and considered them analogs. A complicating factor is that as you experiment, you may actually *dream* of leaving the body.

With practice, however, you should be able to tell the difference. Some telltale signs may help you to discriminate between these two levels of mental experience. Celia Green, who has made an in-depth study of lucid dreaming as well as the OBE, sums them up as follows:

1.   *The OBE usually occurs from a waking state or upon waking from a dream, while a lucid dream usually evolves from more normal dreaming.*

2.   *The lucid dreamer often finds incongruities in the dream environment; the OBer usually experiences him- or herself in a consistent environment, as if he or she were in the real world.**

*This is not an absolute principle, since incongruities are known to occur while one is out-of-body. For instance, a normally dark room may seem perfectly illuminated. But the environment will be much more self-consistent than a dream world tends to be.

3. *Lucid dreams often include fantastic dreamlike elements. Most conventional OBEs are rather mundane.*

4. *OBEs are usually experienced as more vivid, "real," and emotionally intense than lucid dreams, which, no matter how aware one becomes in time, remain dreams.*

5. *The lucid dreamer invariably experiences him- or herself as possessing a body, while many OBers find themselves disembodied.*

To repeat what was said at the beginning of this chapter, another point of difference is how one experiences him- or herself while undergoing a lucid dream. The average lucid dreamer experiences the dream body as his or her only form. Although the lucid dreamer may levitate and fly about, usually there is no true awareness that his or her real physical body is "somewhere else." A person undergoing an OBE is usually deeply aware of having separated from his or her physical body. He or she *thinks* about this body, which the lucid dreamer does not. This sense of being away from the physical body, which may be resting miles away, is a definite attribute of the OBE. I have had, for instance, several nocturnal OBEs while out of town on business. Usually I just suddenly "find" myself back in my home in Los Angeles with no awareness of actually having left the body. On each occasion, the experience has been accompanied by the initial reaction of "What am I doing here? My body is in New York [or wherever I happened to be visiting]!" This awareness of virtual separation from the body always alerts me to my out-of-body state and rarely occurs during simple lucid dreaming. For this reason, I also think that many of Van Eeden's initial "lucid dreams" were actually OBEs.

In the long run, however, you will be able to tell the difference between a dream and an OBE with experience. Then this whole issue will seem academic to you.

REFERENCES

Arnold-Forster, Mary. *Studies in Dreams.* London: Allen & Unwin, 1921.

Fox, Oliver (Hugh Callaway). *Astral Projection.* New Hyde Park, N.Y.: University Books, 1962 (reprint).

Garfield, Patricia. *Creative Dreaming.* New York: Random House, 1974.

_____. *Pathway to Ecstasy.* New York: Holt, Rinehart & Winston 1979.

Green, Celia. *Lucid Dreams.* Oxford, England: Institute of Psychophysical Research, 1968.

Muldoon, Sylvan, and Carrington, Hereward. *The Projection of the Astral Body.* London: Rider, 1929.

Ouspensky, P. D. *A New Model of the Universe.* London: Routledge & Kegan Paul, 1960 (reprint).

Van Eeden, Frederick. A study of dreams. *Proceedings of the Society for Psychical Research,* 1913, *26,* 431-61.

Whiteman, J. H. M. *The Mystical Life.* London: Faber & Faber, 1961.

chapter nine
Projection Through Guided Imagery

A fascinating psychological technique called "guided imagery" or "the waking dream" merges visualization skills with a self-programmed reverie. The procedure involves guiding a meditating subject into an exploration of his or her own unconscious mind by suggesting that the person experience open-ended mental journeys. Each phase of the journey symbolizes a different aspect of the participant's life. The subject responds by reporting the spontaneous imagery that arises as he or she surveys each level of the hypnagogiclike environment. Since the OBE seems inherently related to relaxation, visualization skills, and presleep imagery, the waking dream method might be a plausible approach to its induction. Although no well-known astral projectors of the past or present have used or even suggested guided imagery techniques, the basic technique of the waking dream can be readily adapted for such use. One midwestern psychologist is currently using such an approach and is claiming much success with it.

BACKGROUND

The modern use of guided imagery techniques has quite a history. When Freud discovered the "talking cure" of psychoanalysis, his breakthrough revolutionized our conception and understanding of the unconscious. Freud's discovery that access to our unconscious minds can be gained through free association, by observing slips of the tongue, and through verbalized dream recall were pre-eminent achievements. Freud's approach had one great drawback, however. In emphasizing the verbal description and component of our mental lives, psychoanalysis ostracized the crucial role that mental imagery can play in our search for self-understanding. The psychoanalysts banned the inner world of daydreaming, creative imagery, and hypnagogic experience—along with demons and cold water baths—as viable approaches to mental health and self-discovery.

Luckily, not all turn-of-the-century psychotherapists rushed to join the psychoanalytic bandwagon. Several psychologists in France and Germany realized that mental imagery might represent an alternative key to the unconscious mind. These researchers appreciated the fact that when experiencing a spontaneous mental image during therapy, the patient was dealing with a nonverbal and primordial communication system—that is, direct messages from the unconscious, often conveying ideas or inner experiences that the patient could not even begin to express in words. These images allowed the astute therapist to grasp what was going on inside the patient's head, without having to wade through the defensive interpretations and maskings that a client would so often employ when verbally describing his or her conflicts and problems. Before long a few brave clinicians began trying to induce mental imagery in their patients in hopes of using these mental pictures as an aid to psychotherapy.

One of these pioneers was the German therapist Carl Happich, who worked with what he called "emergent images." He would train his patients to relax, learn to breathe steadily and rhythmically, and meditate. Happich considered any resulting mental imagery as direct messages from the unconscious. To stimulate the production of this imagery, he would suggest that his patients go on mental journeys to various locations—such as to a prairie, a mountain, a flowing stream, and so on. He believed that he could actually change his patients' behavior patterns by working directly with the associated images that appeared during these guided tours. This idea was later extended by another German therapist, Wolfgang Kretschner, who induced similar "landscape" images in his patients. Kretschner considered any associated images that surfaced to be symbolic of internal psychic problems. The goal was to show a patient how to gain access to his or her own unconscious mind and the symbols contained within it—a perfect road to self-discovery.

Yet other pioneers utilized a rather different and much more biological approach to guided imagery. Although he had several predecessors, the most significant of these clinicians was Ludwig Frank. He, too, had discovered that deep relaxation stimulated the emergence of hypnagogic imagery. Greatly influenced by the psychoanalytic claim that one could achieve mental health through the discharge (or catharsis) of unhealthy mental material, he and his followers believed that producing spontaneous mental imagery was a self-normalizing procedure that was automatically cathartic. Therefore, they felt that learning to produce mental imagery was therapeutic in itself.

Meanwhile, a researcher in Switzerland, Marc Guillerey, was experimenting to see if specially suggested mental imagery could help his patients find solutions to their problems. He noted that when his patients were asked to reverie, conflicting images often appeared. He believed that helping them resolve these incongruities would carry over and help them solve real-life problems, which the conflicts no doubt symbolized.

The most systematic research on specific techniques for guided imagery were developed in France at the turn of the century. The pioneer was Eugene Caslant, who would darken his consulting room and teach his patients to travel up and down an imaginary ladder or staircase—symbolizing levels of the patient's unconscious mind. It was almost a form of hypnosis, although no specific suggestions for trance-induction were used.

Caslant's basic technique evolved into what is today called the "directed daydream." The procedure was formally proposed by Robert Desoille, who believed that a patient could be cured of neurotic adaptations by learning to interact with his or her inner mental life. Desoille induced specific imagery in his patients, so that they could learn to confront, evoke, and eventually control even the most threatening images, which were specially chosen to symbolically represent the patient's problems. Desoille took his patients on fantastic journeys in which they traveled down into the ocean or confronted menacing dragons. These symbols, rich in archetypal meaning, are potentially threatening to a great many people. Desoille worked with his patients until they could confront these psychoactive symbols without fear or anxiety. More than any other researcher before him, with the exception of C. G. Jung, Desoille realized that images and symbols are the virtual language of the unconscious—symbols that can be used to implement psychological change.

Much of this same type of work was carried on by Hanscarl Leuner in Germany, who developed a system known as "guided affective imagery." This system helps the client to free the imagination, define mental problems, and even check on the course of his or her psychological change during the course of therapy. The actual techniques are quite extensive, but the basic process begins with teaching the patient to imagine neutral or positive mental pictures. The patient is then taken on imaginary journeys where he or she has to handle more threatening experiences. A female client, for instance, might be taken to a deserted roadside where she must confront a motorist in a symbolic representation of a sexual encounter. The imagery invoked during the waking dream will alert the therapist to problems the patient is facing in real life, as well as possible solutions to them.

Although each of these researchers used slightly different approaches to the induction of mental imagery and guided reverie, they all worked from a basic premise: our mental imagery can have a profound effect on our waking lives. By working with a patient's imagery, one can also change the person.

At least one researcher today believes that this change can include learning to completely divorce the consciousness from the body. Sandor Brent, a developmental psychologist by training, designed his techniques as an adjunct to more conventional sensitivity training. Originally working with several experimental workshops at Wayne State University in Detroit, Brent began experimenting with imagery exercises several years ago as a way to help people learn control over their mental experiences. This training included having the students construct an imaginary trip into outer space. Brent soon found that after being guided through the voyage, some of his subjects reported experiences very similar to classical OBEs and near-death encounters. This discovery led the psychologist to reformulate his exercises specifically as a formal OBE induction technique, although his program is basically designed for group and not individual use.

THE TECHNIQUE

Since Sandor Brent has worked with only large classes of participants, his technique would be somewhat awkward to implement on an individual level. His procedures also require the use of a guide to help the participant through the imagery; though a prepared tape may work equally well.

Ideally, a group of students should meet with a trained "tour guide" familiar with the Brent program. Since Brent has published the complete text of one of his imaginary tours (see the references at the end of the chapter), the guide need merely read this material to the group or devise a series of suggestions based on it.

The size of the class may vary, but you should dim the lights, recline on the floor or sit in comfortable chairs, and try to become as relaxed as possible. Just as important as your physical setting is your psychological attitude toward the experiment. It will help if you get together with some fellow travelers and talk for a while, develop mutual trust, and discuss the experiences that may result from the guided imagery.

Once you have stabilized your physical and psychological milieu, the actual induction phase may begin. Your group leader should start by appealing to your intellectual powers and then gradually guide your attention to a more experiential level, speaking in a slow, soft, and calm tone of voice. The guide should not speak as though reading the instructions, but should extemporize as he or she guides you. Brent, for example, always speaks extemporaneously, but he builds his remarks around a tightly architectured sequence of suggestions.

1. *The guide explains that you are about to experience a world of mental life "out there" in the real world and not merely inside your head. He or she instructs you to observe the room in which you are located and consider how people normally view the outside world as something apart and away from us.*

2. *The guide explains how limited purely physical sight actually is, reminding you that only a tiny peek into the vast spectrum of the physical world is available through the cues we receive from the optical organs. We actually* construct *the environment in which we perceive ourselves through these minimal cues.*

Brent believes that this phase of the program softens psychological resistance to the OBE by helping subjects to realize that there are other avenues of perceptions available to them besides just optical viewing. The next two suggestions continue this softening mode.

3. *The guide now explains how human perceptions are based greatly on our expectations, especially in the way the environment around us is structured.*

4. *The guide reminds you that soon you will be going on an imaginary journey where you will be experiencing perceptions different from any you have had before. You are reminded that you will be incapable of categorizing your experiences. You must accept them for what they are.*

Since you are in a very receptive and passive state during a guided imagery session, all these comments and suggestions will work on an unconscious as well as conscious level. The above suggestions will help you divorce yourself from relying on your critical judgment during your imaginary trip. Critically assessing your experiences may limit your ability to leave the body. Your guided OBE is somewhat akin to the process of remote viewing, during which you must also learn to take a nonjudgmental attitude toward anything you experience.

5. *The guide now reminds you that how you experience your physical body is also a partially subjective experience. It is by habit that we associate our minds as "in" the body and cut off from direct interaction with the outside world. This habit can be broken with practice.*

6. *Now the guide tells you to move your focus of awareness to different locations in the body, suggesting that you become aware of each part of the body, shift your consciousness there, and literally experience yourself from that perspective. This transference of consciousness phase should start with the toes and progress through the body to the head. The guide constantly reminds you to momentarily intensify and then simply "release" the tension you may find at any body location.*

7. *You are next instructed to scan your body mentally and locate any areas that are sites of residual tension. Release the tension through mental massage.*

At this point, of course, Brent seems to be drawing on some basic procedures known to enhance OBE capabilities. Muldoon also suggested the practice of having the student shift the location of his or her awareness, though he advised the student to focus on the heartbeat. This procedure seems to help in letting go the normal inclination to associate awareness with purely cerebral functions. Along with it, releasing tension in the body induces a form of deep relaxation that helps induce mental imagery. These procedures could well induce mind/body releases in some people.

After this lengthy preparatory phase is over, the OBE phase of the session begins.

8. *The guide instructs you to leave the body by projecting through the head.*

9. *You are instructed to stand next to your body and inspect it.*

At this point, your guide can instruct you to carry out any out-of-body task he or she pleases, as decided by a previous decision of the group. Brent uses an OBE voyage into outer space, since this aids the student to experience a more defined separation from the body and teaches the person, through the use of his or her observations, to think in nonanalytical terms. Since the student will be experiencing new sights and sounds, he or she will not be tempted to base perceptions on past experiences.

10. *Your guide instructs you to leave the room and the building.*

11. *Now you are asked to rise into the air until you can see the landscape beneath you.*

12. *The guide urges that you propel yourself into outer space and suggests images—such as planets and star patterns—that you might see while looking back at the earth.*

13. *The trip ends as your instructor guides you to a great void or white light.*

In the first experiments, Brent ended the guided imagery at this point. This caused some confusion for students who found themselves deeply engrossed in their imaginary trips or who had induced spontaneous OBEs. Since some subjects had a hard time reorienting to their bodies or "finding their way back," Brent revised his procedure to include the following phases:

14. *You are instructed to begin your descent to earth by reversing your journey.*

15. *You are asked to find your body back where you left it.*

16. *The trip ends as the guide suggests that you merge with your body again and wake up.*

The session should formally conclude with a good debriefing, which might include sharing your experiences and reactions to the procedure with the group. As Brent proposes, the participants should be "encouraged to share both the pleasant and unpleasant aspects of the experience, as well as to discuss whether or not they even had any significant experience at all as a result of the instructions." Questionnaires might be given out asking what kind of experiences the participants had, to what depth they found themselves out-of-body, whether they found it pleasant, and so on. (A copy of Brent's own suggested questionnaire may be found in his published description of the program.)

COMMENTS

Since a transcription of one of Brent's own guided sessions would take well over 10 pages, this description has been necessarily brief. It would even be impractical to give a detailed *summary* of a typical guided session, nor does this seem to be important. Brent himself talks extemporaneously, so each of his sessions varies. The only critical part of the procedure is for the guide to arrange suggestions in a specific order to break down your habitual ways of thinking, free the mind from the way you normally think about it, relax you, and then guide you out of the body. This procedure makes considerable practical sense, since the use of mental suggestion to relax, dehabituate your thought processes, shift thinking from concrete to a more experiential level, and interact with mental imagery are all apparently related to the ability to induce the OBE. Brent's habit of appealing to the intellect, then gradually turning the participant's attention toward more experientially oriented considerations also might be of great value in divorcing one's self from the body.

On the other hand, Brent's guided imagery techniques have their own share of problems. The procedure may activate your imagination, but it does little to help develop imagery skills. You are told to use your imagery abilities, but you are given no instructions as how best to proceed. This is an essential component when visualization of any kind is used as an adjunct to the OBE. Brent also places more emphasis on experiencing the body than actually relaxing it. During the initial phases of the induction, a student's attention may become virtually riveted to the body, thus inhibiting him or her from leaving it.

These are all basically academic matters, however, since a few experiments have actually been conducted to determine how efficacious the

Brent procedure really is. Brent conducted one such experiment himself at Wayne State University while preparing his protocol for formal publication. The session was held in an upper-story classroom with 45 students participating. Over one-half of them were between 19 and 23 years old, and the majority were psychology majors. Most were naive to the system, and only a relative few had ever gone through any sort of "altered states of consciousness" induction procedure. Well over half the participants claimed no familiarity with the OBE. Brent took the entire class, who were asked to sit in typical classroom chairs, on an imaginary OBE voyage to outer space and back. At the conclusion of the session, he passed out questionnaires asking the students whether they had left the body, to what degree they felt separated, whether they found the experience pleasant, and what background they had in exploring altered states of consciousness.

His results were fairly impressive. Twelve volunteers claimed that they had been able to get "part way through the body," while five others reported full OBEs. A large number (18) explained that they did not feel as if they had actively left the body, but had indeed experienced themselves way out in space. The majority of the respondents found the guided imagery enjoyable. Those who were able to merge deepest with the experience of being out-of-body consistently rated the experience as more pleasant than those who had a more superficial response.

Some of the experiential reports Brent collected also read like fairly typical OBEs. "The most vivid moment," writes one student, "was that in which I 'stood' behind myself and viewed the silent class. The feeling of soaring through space was difficult to achieve, but my imagination was at its height when I was asked to float into nothingness. Returning to my body was not difficult, but I felt a positive relief at my consciousness again being seated within my body."

So reminiscent of the experiences of the great historical astral projectors was the response of one psychology major who wrote, "Amazing ... I have never put my body on like a glove before." Or another who exclaimed, "I really didn't want to come back."

Brent naturally feels that his procedure holds great promise for the academic study of the OBE, and concludes that this experiment fully confirms and validates the usefulness of his system.

But have other experimenters been successful with this method? The variable with any procedure using a guide or instructor is the charisma and influence he or she contributes to the session. Guided imagery is similar to hypnosis in that rapport between subject and inducer can play a crucial role in the nature of the subsequent results. Brent obviously brings a sense of enthusiasm to his classes. He enjoys actually going out of his body along with them and likes to interact with the students long before the session begins. What he achieves through the use of guided imagery may be much more than what a disinterested or less enthusiastic leader might obtain.

At least two independent experimenters have tried to replicate Brent's work, and their results may be a truer indication of the success of the Brent system. The first was Janet Mitchell, who ran a Brent-style session at the American Society for Psychical Research as part of a five-week seminar on parapsychology. Dr. Mitchell recruited eight volunteers for a formal experiment conducted in two rooms in the A.S.P.R.'s three-story New York townhouse. The volunteers relaxed in a downstairs room while Mitchell read Brent's entire procedure to them—up to the point where they were to leave the body. She then guided them out of the body and tried to direct them telepathically to an upstairs room where a special viewing box had been set up. (A picture could be seen if a participant stood directly in front of the box and peeked through a viewing hole.)

None of the subjects were able to report the target picture correctly. The volunteers were later taken to the room, and few of them recollected having actually traveled there. Nor did most of them particularly like the procedure, feeling that the induction instructions made them focus on their bodies too much, or merely made them sleepy.

It might have helped if the subjects had been shown the room before the session began. Perhaps they should also have been deliberately told to go there while out-of-body. But the fact that Mitchell's subjects had a rather uniformly negative reaction to the session stands in striking contrast to Brent's own results.

Another attempt to employ the Brent procedure was carried out by Dr. Gertrude Schmeidler, a psychologist and parapsychologist at the City University of New York, as part of a seminar she was giving for the Spiritual Frontiers Fellowship in Virginia. This organization's membership is interested in the interface between religion and psychical research, and most of the seminar group (of between 30 to 40 people) claimed prior OBEs or other psychic experiences. They met in a large assembly room where the Brent procedures were read to them. After instructing the participants to leave the body, Schmeidler directed them to enter an adjoining room where two target pictures had been (unbeknownst to them) placed on a shelf. The subjects were asked to look at the pictures and remember them before returning to the body. One target was a large "S" written on a piece of cardboard; the other was a similar cardboard poster printed with a reddish square.

Because of the group's prior interest in developing psychic ability, Dr. Schmeidler was not too surprised when practically all the volunteers reported full or partial OBEs. Some even reported difficulties getting back into the body. Only two or three, however, were able to see and report the targets correctly.

So at present, the evidence for the efficacy of Brent's particular type of guided imagery is at a stalemate. Although many people *experience* themselves out-of-body as a result of the induction, there seems little formal documentation that they have actually separated from their bodies. This is the problem most experimenters who have toyed with OBE induction procedures have had to face. Dr. Palmer ran into this very same problem during his University of Virginia project. Yet, this does not mean that Brent's guided imagery is worthless. Dr. Schmeidler's results suggest that as a result of the Brent program, at least a few people are able to make correct observations about distant locations. So while some people may be incited to fantasize that they are out-of-body, others may be able to make more efficient use of the system.

Although the cogency of Brent's procedures are somewhat questionable, this does not mean that guided imagery in general is a fruitless approach to the OBE either. Perhaps other forms of guided imagery might work better.

During the summer of 1981, I decided to experiment with a guided imagery procedure partially adapted from Brent's, when a private parapsychology group invited me to lead a discussion on the OBE and then organize some sort of informal experiential exercise. The use of a guided imagery procedure was a natural choice.

When I met with the group a week later in a private home in Los Angeles, I found that they ranged in age from the early twenties to the late forties. All reported previous psychic experiences and had a strong interest in developing their abilities further. This made them a perfect group for my purposes, since they were very open and excited about the prospect of undergoing an OBE. Two participants reported previous spontaneous OBEs, while one woman had undergone a particularly dramatic near-death OBE as a result of a severe accidental electrical shock. The fact that only three out of the 18 members had undergone previous OBEs indicated to me that the group was fairly typical in their collective "OBE talent threshold," since this percentage (16) is roughly equivalent to the portion of the general population reporting OBEs.

While talking with the participants, however, it became clear that few of them had made any particular study of the OBE. Most had experimented with "altered states of consciousness" of one sort or another, such as hypnosis or meditation, but they were generally naive about out-of-body travel.

The workshop began with an informal talk/discussion in which we chatted about the nature of the OBE. I followed Brent's advice about mutual sharing and trust and encouraged the participants to speak about their previous experiences and feelings about out-of-body travel. Sometimes I interrupted the discussion to offer some concrete information about the experience or to answer specific questions posed by the group. I also informed them about current research on the OBE, gave them historical techniques for inducing the experiences, and offered some statistics about how commonly the experience is reported by the general public. After the discussion we enjoyed a leisurely coffee break during which I, along with the group leaders, set up the experimental portion of the workshop.*

All participants were instructed to lie down on the floor or on the couches available in the room where we were meeting. Following several leads suggested by Palmer's research, I decided to induce a ganzfeld setting as an adjunct to the guided imagery strategy, since sensory isolation seems to help induce OBEs. Setting up a group ganzfeld is not the easiest thing to do when you have close to 20 people on your hands, but Dr. Moss and I had come prepared with several halved ping-pong balls, transparent tape, and wads of cotton. It was not long before we had the entire group lying down on their backs and staring at the ceiling through their makeshift goggles. As one of the participants quipped, at least I had successfuly induced a "Little Orphan Annie" experience in everyone! I also supplied the lights in the room with low-wattage red bulbs, so that everyone would be staring at a blank reddish visual field. The home in which we were meeting was located fairly near a freeway, so the rather homogeneous background

*I would like to thank Dr. Thelma Moss, formerly of the U.C.L.A. Neuropsychiatric Institute, and Dr. Jan Berlin for the opportunity to work with their group and for helping me prepare and run the session.

noise of the distant traffic—augmented by a chorus of home-grown California crickets—served nicely to produce an unpatterned auditory field.

Since I wanted to experimentally validate any OBEs that might result from the session, I used the coffee break to slip into an adjoining
room where I placed a target picture on a coffee table. This picture was
one of many I use for ESP testing, which I keep sealed in individual envel-
opes. I had no idea which picture I had brought with me and placed it on
the table without looking at it. No one knew I was going to incorporate an
ESP test as part of the workshop, and I made sure that no one entered the
room before the test session began.

With all the preparations made and everyone ready to go, I guided
the group through a revised version of the Brent procedures. This included
having the participants question the objectivity of their perceptions and
having them transfer awareness to different locations in their bodies. I
gradually worked up to the point where they would be asked to leave the
body. I suggested that they leave through the head, look at their own
bodies, and then go to the next room and look at the target I had placed
there. I suggested that those subjects who had not yet left the body give
themselves the mental suggestion that they would indeed project when
they were ready to. There followed a 20-minute period of silence during
which I allowed the subjects to explore their OBEs—or try to experience
one.

At the end of this period, I followed Brent's suggestions by having the
participants retrace their steps back to the body and re-enter. The session
was then terminated.

Everyone seemed relaxed by the exercise and began reorienting themselves while stripping off the ping-pong balls. During this "return to normal" adjustment period, I scooted into the adjoining room and placed the
target picture back in its envelope. Once again I refrained from peeking at
it. (Fumbling around in a strange room can be lots of fun. There *are*
practical problems in running experiments like this, but luckily I have very
good imagery and had memorized the room's layout upon first entering
it.) Then I returned to the experimental area for a group debriefing. Five
of the participants, four of them women, felt they had undergone OBEs.
This means that 22 percent of the volunteers had successfully merged with
the guided imagery, a rate not inconsistent with Brent's own findings.
While all of the successful participants had made it into the adjoining
room, most of them experienced some difficulty focusing on the target.
One woman thought it depicted something like a carpet with a red banner.

Another could only describe it as a white field with a red streak against it. Both descriptions impressed me, since the target picture turned out to be a color picture of an American flag waving in the wind.*

Since I was not able to collect written accounts from these five participants, I could not compare their experiences to more spontaneously encountered OBEs. Thus, I could not substantiate Brent's claim that OBEs induced through guided imagery are indistinguishable from, or at least closely resemble, spontaneous ones.

Now it could be argued that this experiment was in no way a replication of the Brent work since I made several revisions to it. However, I was not really interested in conducting a formal replication of Brent's specific techniques. My suggestions were modeled after Brent's and contained nothing antagonistic to them, but I was more concerned with determining whether guided imagery can be used for successful OBE induction in general.

All in all, I found the results of my test encouraging and would eventually like to see more formal and controlled experimentation done on guided imagery as a possible road to the OBE.

For the student who wishes to practice out-of-body travel, however, any sort of guided imagery procedure is going to be cumbersome in the long run. You really cannot use this technique on your own, but need a friend or guide who can lead you through it. Even the use of a recorded tape does away with the potentially important role social interactions or mental rapport plays in preparing you for the experience of being out-of-body. So, although an interesting technique, guided imagery will probably not rank very highly as you consider various approaches to your self-development and experimentation.

REFERENCES

Brent, Sandor. Deliberately induced pre-mortem, out-of-body experiences: An experiential and theoretical approach. In *Between Life and Death*, Robert Kastenbaum, ed. New York: Springer, 1979.

---

*I also made a statistical evaluation of how well these descriptions compared with those participants who had not left the body but had received impressions through "normal" ESP. The OBers were more successful, but several biasing factors could have influenced the scoring.

Epstein, Gerald. *Waking Dream Therapy.* New York: Human Sciences
    Press, 1981.
Mitchell, Janet. Personal communication to the author (January 1982).
Schmeidler, Gertrude. Personal communications to the author (January
    1982).
Watkins, Mary. *Waking Dreams.* New York: Gordon & Breach, 1976.

chapter ten
Of What Use Is Astral Projection?

You have finally been able to leave the body. What should you do now? To what *use* can you put the phenomenon? Is there really any good in merely floating away from the body now and then?

The answer is yes. The OBE is a unique phenomenon that can teach us much about the nature of life and reality. It should be used as a teaching aid and not as a goal unto itself. But before exploring these complex issues, there are more basic ones that must be resolved. Do the techniques outlined in this book really work? Is any one technique better than any other? Is the OBE an hallucination, or a genuine separation of the mind from the body? Before going any further, these questions—which may have been nagging at you as you read this book—should be answered as directly as possible.

My own feeling is that *all* the techniques outlined here will work. There is evidence that at least a few people have learned out-of-the-body travel by the use of each one of them. But there is no reason to believe that any particular system is necessarily more efficient than the others. It all comes down to the problem of individual differences. Every person is a unique individual. Someone who has problems controlling his or her mental imagery should veer away from visualization techniques. Anyone who is very poor at dream recall might reject the idea of using lucid dreams as a catalyst. Others with no aptitude for meditation may not want to bother with yogic techniques.

People who engage in the simple art of meditation have several schools of practice and thought from which to choose, including zen, TM, yoga, Sufism, and many others. A person's own individual psychology will draw that individual to the system to which he or she can best adapt. The same holds true for the OBE.

It is also likely that most of these systems work for the same reason. It is not so much the technique that is critical, but the attitude and desire of the practitioner. Certainly there must be physical factors that help. The universal emphasis on lying down on the back, relaxing the body, and remaining in a quiet place, taught by all OBE induction systems, is probably telling us something very important. But it seems likely that the will and desire to have an OBE is the crucial factor that makes these systems work. OBE induction techniques might best be viewed as focusing devices to help centralize and intensify the will. The great Western occultists of the Victorian Age appear to have intuitively grasped this idea. Their advice, to practice and imagine leaving the body until it finally happens, is based on this very premise. They realized that you will have an OBE only when you are (unconsciously) prepared to have one. There is also circumstantial evidence that the unconscious mind regulates the OBE and that various induction methods serve as only a secondary contribution to successful astral projection. Note now many techniques were developed to help the student become OBE-prone, not that he or she would be able to project at will as a result of their execution. Note, too, how many people encounter their first OBEs when they least expect it and/or have ceased practicing for the day, week, or even permanently. Once again we see the tricky hand of the unconscious at work.

If there is a great secret to leaving the body, it is that practice serves to dynamize the unconscious will. Induction techniques are forms of ritualized self-suggestion.

In this respect, astral projection is very much like any "magical" practice. The great initiates freely advised their students to practice ceremonial magic to bring about prescribed events in the world. The goal might be to obtain unexpected money, or merely to make someone change a behavior or attitude; but reading between the lines, it is plain that these practitioners recognized the human will as the primary key to magic. They also realized that a person is able to use powers of ESP and mind-over-matter to bring about events in the "real" world of the five senses. They knew, too, that rituals focus attention, ingrain the wish in the unconscious mind, and serve as a dynamic form of auto-suggestion. When a magical ritual does work, it is because the practitioner's mind has activated his or her own unconscious ESP or psychokinetic abilities. The ritual serves basically as a means of contacting the inner mind and its vast potentials.

Even a few parapsychologists have begun to accept a similar view in their own work. Many procedures for helping people gain access to their ESP abilities—such as ganzfeld stimulation or formal hypnotic induction— might also be considered simple magical rituals. In other words, the experimenter (magically) does something to his or her subjects that makes them *believe* they will be able to tap their hidden psychic talents. These procedures probably work because *we believe* they work—and can make our subjects believe it, too. This acts auto-suggestively on the unconscious mind, the seat of psychic ability. Whether one calls this effect "expectancy set" or simply "placebo" makes no difference. The results may still be due to activation of the unconscious.

There has been one attempt to test this theory experimentally. A bright young student at the (former) division of parapsychology and psychophysics at Maimonides Medical Center in Brooklyn, New York, designed a test that actually incorporated the use of a magical ritual. The "sender" was kept in one room and given a target picture to transmit to a friend in another chamber down the hall. As the agent sent the target, he was asked to engage in a voodoo-like ritual that included lighting candles and staring at occult symbols. The college student who designed this interesting test did not believe in voodoo or magic as such, but he theorized that the ritual would help dynamize the agent's will and focus his attempt at sending the target. It was meant to appeal to the agent's mind on a primitive, magical level. Unfortunately, the experiment was never completed, so we do not yet know if the student was really onto something.

There may be, however, exceptions to this auto-suggestive theory about the nature of OBE induction techniques. Some procedures may indeed help a person *after he or she has first developed the ability to project;* they may, therefore, serve as tools rather than as roads to the OBE. There is also a good possibility that yogic breathing induces certain energy changes in the body, which help release the consciousness from its confines.

If you have successfully left the body, however, you might still be puzzled by the basic nature of your experience, and still harbor lingering doubts about what you have undergone. Have you really left the body, or have you merely suffered a momentary hallucination? The lessons we have learned through *normal* reality testing and through the collected wisdom of our culture are hard to abandon.

Parapsychologists are far from sure just what the OBE represents. Most of my colleagues, judging from conversations with them, tend to believe that the OBE is a psychological experience and nothing more. Of course, they readily admit that some people can "travel" to distant locations during the OBE, "see" what is going on there, and then corroborate it all. But perhaps, these parapsychologists argue, the OBE is a special type of hallucination during which one makes ready use of ESP. In the long run, however, no purely psychological theory—no matter how far we extend it—can really explain the OBE and its many complexities.

Take the most common explanation, that the OBE is merely a dream in which the dreamer makes occasional use of ESP. This naive concept has been unequivocally disproved. Several brain-wave studies made with such projectors as Keith Harary and Ingo Swann during their out-of-body voyages have conclusively shown that these men are definitely *not* asleep and dreaming when they leave the body.

Then there is the idea that the OBE is a quirk of perception; a perceptual jump during which a person momentarily *thinks* he or she is out of body and uses memory to reconstruct an environment consistent with this new perspective. This is all very clever, but why then do most projectors have definite experiences of leaving and returning to the body, when undergoing an OBE—including buzzing in the ears, bodily vibration, and even shock and/or pain upon returning? A purely psychological version of the perceptual-jump theory would predict that the person would experience the OBE as a sudden "jump" from within his or her body to a point outside it. But that rarely happens to many habitual projectors.

Yet a third theory is that the OBE results from a disturbance in one's awareness of the body. The foremost supporter of this view is Dr. John Palmer, who believes that an OBE occurs when the subject experiences a marked alteration in proprioceptive feedback. This causes the individual to become unconsciously anxious, since his or her body is being experienced in an anomalous way. This in turn causes a threat to the subject's concept of "self." In order to re-establish self-identity, the subject experiences him- or herself as totally out-of-body, even constructing an apparitional body. This really is not a very satifying resolution, Palmer goes on to argue, so the projector soon finds him- or herself back in the body as normal defenses take over. Palmer believes that this theory can account for the OBE, whether it is considered an hallucination or a genuine mind/body release. His own personal view, however, is that the OBE is most likely an hallucination, although perhaps an especially ESP-conducive one.

Yet even this tightly evolved theory cannot explain why some people can nurture direct control over the OBE. Nor can it explain why some people have one spontaneous experience after another. If, as Palmer points out, the OBE is an unsatisfactory means of resolving the threat to the self, then a person who has undergone one or two such experiences would quickly develop more successful ways of dealing with such threats and would stop having the experience altogether. After all, the unconscious mind would learn in time that these so-called threats to the self are essentially harmless.

So, only some sort of true separation theory can account for the OBE. But is there any real *use* for such an experience?

One of the OBE's most fundamental values is what it teaches about our minds and our spiritual nature. As with so many others who have left the body, I share the view that the OBE is a literal "rehearsal" for death, an experience that actively demonstrates the principle of personal immortality. It is not by mere linguistic fancy that the OBE voyages of the shamans are called "flights of the soul." They show us that some part of the mind and personality can function independently of the body and might well survive it. The out-of-body state seems so much more vivid, primal, and real than existence in the physical world that many people who have left look back upon their bodies with total indifference. And not even the most skeptical psychologist or parapsychologist would deny that a person who has had an OBE adopts a new attitude toward death itself.

This is especially true of indivuduals who have had OBEs during heart attacks or while confronting other life-threatening situations. Formal research has found that people who survive near-death encounters experience a marked reduction of normal death anxiety. Dr. Michael Sabom, a cardiologist at Emory University in Georgia, has taken this finding one step further by discovering that this reduction occurs *only* in those people who specifically have OBEs while actually nearing death. It is *not* found in those people who merely have close brushes with death.

There is now scientific evidence that having spontaneous OBEs dramatically reduces death anxiety as well. When Robert Monroe was given a personality assessment at the Topeka V.A. Hospital, his clinicians concluded that "compared with a normal population, [his] anxiety and fear of death [are] very low." They also found that Monroe possessed "no evidence of fear of imminent death, or an attempt to deny death." This same finding cropped up when Drs. Jones, Twemlow, and Gabbard initiated their wide-ranging Kansas project in 1976. After conducting an intensive mail survey, they found that many respondents viewed the OBE as "a spiritual or religious experience, an experience of great beauty and lasting benefit, and affected a change toward belief in life after death."

This "instructional nature" of the OBE has carried over into other areas of research. Dr. Kenneth Ring of the University of Connecticut at Storrs was the first to scientifically document the fact that people who have OBEs at the point of death show a marked reduction of death anxiety. Ring also found that people who know something about the OBE tend *not* to leave the body when menaced by life-threatening situations. "Naive" people have them much more commonly. One interpretation of this odd finding is that the OBE is a teaching aid our minds use to convince us of our personal immortality. A person familiar with the OBE may not need to be convinced of the fact, so he or she does not undergo the experience in the face of a life-threatening accident or illness.

All this has an obvious bearing on the potential use of OBE induction. Palmer sums it up best in the April 1974 issue of the *Osteopathic Physician* when he writes, "the experience may have practical applications as well. Many people who have had striking OBEs report that the experience convinced them of survival after death and eliminated their fear of death. Whether or not this conclusion can be considered subjectively valid, it does suggest some therapeutic possibilities for the OBE. For example, the experience may help persons in occupations where there is a genuine risk of death and where fear of the danger may adversely affect their performance. Finally, the experience might be useful in treating an irrational fear of death in certain psychiatric patients."

Perhaps the OBE could be used to help terminal patients preoccupied with their own deaths. Learning to leave the body could be used to combat the overwhelming sense of depression and despair these people so often face. When not even strong medication can deliver the dying patient from physical pain, perhaps the OBE might be induced as a respite from such agony. In any event, a person who has successfully left the body will be better prepared for death than someone who has not.

There are also less terminal uses of the OBE. Such an experience can genuinely help us to better appreciate and enjoy our earthly lives. The Kansas team found that many of their respondents had used their OBEs for just this type of psychological gain. They had used the experience to help reaffirm their religious beliefs, view life as meaningful, and give themselves a sense of personal value in an otherwise dehumanizing world.

Certainly this is an experience of great psychological worth.

Many people who have undergone the OBE are also enthralled by the aesthetic qualities of the experience. The sense of euphoria and wellbeing experienced during the state is one reason alone for inducing it. The OBE can also profoundly alter our state of consciousness and allow us to peer into the very nature of reality itself.

People who undergo a psychological "peak" experience—during which they blissfully merge with all humanity and creation—universally describe the dramatic impact it has on the way they view the nature of life. They tend to appreciate life more, gain a greater respect for the lives of others, and adopt a much more mentally healthy attitude toward the act of living. This unique and much sought after experience tends to occur more naturally when we are out-of-body than when we are going about our day-to-day activities. The late Dr. Robert Crookall points this out in his book, *The Interpretation of Cosmic and Mystical Experiences;* while Dr. Raynor Johnson, an English physicist who taught at Melbourne University in Australia for over 30 years, collected many cases of OBE-induced peak experiences while studying the psychology of mysticism.

One of Johnson's correspondents supplied him with the following account of an OBE-ignited peak experience:

> *It was on a night in October about eleven P.M. I suddenly found myself out of the body floating over a Highland moor, in a body as light or lighter than air. There was a wood at the side of the moor and the clouds were drifting past the moon and a cool fresh wind was flowing. I found that I didn't mind the wind as I should have done had I been in my physical body, because I was at one with it. The life in the wind and the clouds and the trees was within me also, flowing into me and through me, and I offered no resistance to it. I was filled with glorious life. All the time, in the margin of my consciousness, I knew where my earthly body was, and that I could return to it instantly if danger threatened. The experience may have lasted a few minutes or a few seconds, I cannot tell—for I was outside*

time. I came back greatly invigorated and refreshed, and very much alive. I remember thinking that if this was what the so-called dead experience, how much more vitally alive they are than we are here.

Compare the above account to the following, also collected and published by Dr. Johnson:

It was a hot summer evening. I lay on the lawn in the back garden trying to get cool. The sun had almost set and I watched the planets appear. Suddenly I felt my head swelling. It seemed to increase in size until it contained the whole world: all the stars too. Everything that had ever happened or would happen was within myself. I was in my eighth year at the time, so knew little of history and nothing of religion. I saw many things, events I later learned about, also much I have as yet been able to discover from any physical source. After what seemed untold ages I became aware of my mother telling me to come inside. There was a brief glimpse of my body lying on the grass with my mother bending over it. Then I was awake feeling very bewildered. It was some time before I recovered.

After all these years I still refer to that experience whenever I want to verify anything I hear of or read about. There is always a sense that all happenings are right and in accordance with plan.

These OBEs certainly had a dramatic impact on the people who experienced them. Think how your own life, and your attitude toward it, would be changed by such an experience. You could use it as an aid in the quest to understand the meaning of personal existence, and you could use it to explore the very nature of reality in all its complexities.

And with this discovery, a more esoteric side of the OBE can be unveiled. What I'm about to say here may not go down very well with my fellow parapsychologists, who usually take a very ultraconservative stand about such matters. But then, I have been able to explore the OBE personally, while most of them have not! Although I have not been able to explore it as deeply or intensively as I would have liked, I have at least been alerted to some of the experience's great possibilities and potentials.

I am talking about using the OBE to explore new levels of reality, new dimensions of time and space within the universe. All of the great astral projectors have been aware of these spheres of existence, these "higher worlds," and have glimpsed them. Hugh Callaway, Marcel Louis Forham, Robert Monroe, J. H. M. Whiteman, and many others have described these parallel worlds and spiritual dimensions in their autobiographies. Some have been able to interact with their residents. Keith Harary has personally told me about these "higher worlds" and their inhabitants, and Sylvan Muldoon, who says virtually nothing about them in his own writings, no doubt contacted them occasionally. (I base this claim on some brief and cryptic correspondence I had with him shortly before his death in 1971.) Many parapsychologists would prefer to believe that these dimensions are merely inner worlds created by and within the mind. I disagree. I contend that they are real but metaethereal planes of existence that interface with our own, but that can be contacted only while one is out-of-body.

Realizing this will help us to understand the very structure of the universe and the real purpose to which the OBE can be put. It also helps explain many of the perplexities of the OBE itself.

Both traditional psychology and conventional parapsychology have often looked at the OBE through very myopic eyes. Psychology usually dismisses it as an illusion or mental aberration, and parapsychologists have, by and large, refused to accept that the OBE entails the actual release of some "physical" element of the mind. (They have told me so even when I have discussed my own experiences with them!) Likewise, most conventional laboratory OBE research has been based on some very simplistic assumptions, chiefly that a gifted subject can "travel" in physical space after leaving the body, "look" at some target posters placed in another room or otherwise interact with the "real" world, and report back what he or she has seen. This was the entire basis upon which Dr. Tart, for instance, based his pioneering work. But these assumptions may be wrong.

I began to realize this in 1973 during the research we were conducting with Blue Harary at the Psychical Research Foundation in Durham, North Carolina. Part of the project was designed to see if Blue could project from one building of the P.R.F. complex by Duke University to a neighboring one and make a kitten respond to his presence. The kitten was kept on a shuffleboardlike apparatus where its every movement could be monitored. Many of these tests were completely successful. The kitten was usually very active and would jump and scamper about when placed on the board. But when Blue projected to him, he would hardly move about at all. The contrast was striking.

So far, so good. But when Blue began describing his *own* experiences during the test, the experimenters were in for quite a surprise. After one successful trial, he reported back that he had not been with the cat, but had been caught up in a whole new dimension—a barren, dry, dreamlike world from which he escaped by returning to his body. This surprised everyone, since according to the kitten's behavior, Blue had been at the lab all along. So what happened?

My theory is that Blue's out-of-body consciousness may have indeed been with the kitten somewhat—at least enough for the cat to sense and react to him. But apparently Blue had made simultaneous contact with a new dimension, a metaethereal world intertwining with our own and in which he perceived himself.

This all rather reminds me of Lovecraft's Dunwich Horror, a monster trapped by birth between our world and a fourth-dimensional one. He could not escape his interdimensional prison and was trapped there, although his presence could be felt and perceived. Blue's situation may have been similar. Through the OBE, he had traveled along an interface between our worldly dimension and another one. The cat reacted because it was sensitive enough to feel Blue's ethereal presence, although Blue's consciousness remained more attuned to a vaster dimension.

These experiences are probably more common than one might expect. When you analyze a great many OBE accounts, you gradually realize that the environment in which the projector finds him- or herself is not really the world we normally perceive. It is a mimickry of it. Most people who undergo spontaneous OBEs do not examine their environment closely enough to make this discovery. The usual OBE is all too brief for the projector to examine his or her environment or do a little reality testing. But here and there, a few spontaneous cases do indicate that the typical OBE world is only an imitation of our "real" one.

A well-known American parapsychologist told me he had realized this fact while undergoing a series of OBEs as a college student. "At one time when I was living in Oxford, England, I had an apparent out-of-body experience during the night," he said. "As in most of my other experiences, I only moved around the room in which I was sleeping. The case was somewhat unusual in that the windows had a different set of curtains in my experience than the curtains which were in fact in the room and which I knew to be there. I do not know whether the room ever had the curtains which I 'saw' in my out-of-body experience."

Harary has also had these quixotic encounters. Sometimes he apparently even is able to interact with the OBE world while failing to influence the corresponding physical world. As he once wrote to me:

> *One night I awoke in an out-of-body state floating above my physical body which lay below me on the bed. A candle had been left burning on the other end of the room during the evening. I dove for the candle head first from a sitting position and gently floated down toward it with the intention of blowing out the flame to conserve wax. I put my "face" close to the candle and had some difficulty in putting out the flame. I had to blow on it several times before it finally seemed to extinguish. I turned around, saw my body lying on the bed, and gently floated back into it. Once in the physical [body] I immediately turned over and went back to sleep. The next morning I awoke and found that the candle had completely burned down. It seemed as if my out-of-body efforts had affected only a non-physical candle.*

These revelations relieved me of many doubts I had entertained 10 years before. When I induced my own first OBEs, I could never understand why some of them seemed so "unreal." On one hand, I was sure that I was genuinely out-of-body, yet many incidents had a sort of dreamlike quality to them. During one nocturnal OBE, for instance, I found myself out of my physical body and walking toward the door of my bedroom. I left the room and approached the living room. I saw my two dogs and then realized that a brilliant light was shining. Since it was the middle of the night, the room should have been totally dark; this did not make sense to me. I stopped to figure out the situation, but the distraction caused me to return to the body and awaken.

I got up and checked the living room and, indeed, found it pitch-black. My first thought was that maybe I had been dreaming. Later I theorized that, during a nocturnal OBE, one's perceptions may be colored or influenced by the brain's *normal* dream consciousness.

I had to give up this theory when I met Blue Harary, who has had this same type of anomalous experience during his consciously induced experiences. Rather reluctantly I had to accept the theory that during the OBE, we contact only a *parallel* of the real world—a plastic interactional world that may alter when we physically alter our own. If I place a picture on a wall, for instance, the same object may well appear in the parallel world. But this plane is more tenuous and less stable than the physical world of the five senses, and it wavers and drifts away from a perfect semblance of it. This explains why Blue could sometimes succeed but also occasionally fail to make contact with the physical world during his experimentally induced OBEs. His level of success depended on his ability to maintain an affinity with our world while being drawn simultaneously into a new dimension.

The next questions are obvious: Why don't all of us contact these "higher worlds"? Why do we seem stuck in our familiar environment? One clue comes to us through the experiences and writings of J. H. M. Whiteman of Capetown, South Africa. A physicist by training, Whiteman is also a natural mystic and out-of-body traveler.

According to Professor Whiteman, the universe we normally perceive is only a substructure of a vast realm of dimensions that lie beyond it. These higher worlds can be contacted only psychically. During an OBE, we perceive a mirror image of the real world *because that is what we expect to see.* We are chained to this mirror reality by the limitations of our own minds.

A disciple of Whiteman's, South African biologist Dr. John Poynton, argues that during a student's first OBEs, a close perceptual relationship exists between the OBE environment and the real world. The reason is simple: *the OBer must constantly reassure him- or herself that the experience is real and not a delusion.* The person can do this only by allowing him- or herself to perceive an environment that corresponds to his or her concept of concensus reality.

Not that this is the only environment we may contact during the OBE, however. In time, our minds allow us a peek into new levels of OBE reality. This occurs as the student becomes more at home in the out-of-body world and begins to realize that he or she is not chained to a single dimension but can go on to contact others. This is probably the reason why the great astral projectors have been able to explore planes of existence so few spontaneous projectors ever even dream of.

Many projectors have contacted these dimensions by traveling through apparent holes or tunnels that seem to lead through the very fabric of reality, from one dimension to another. When Hugh Callaway realized that he could escape this world altogether while out-of-body, he searched his OBE environment and quickly spotted one of these "holes in space." He writes how he popped through it and found himself in a whole new dimension of unworldly beauty. Although it resembled the physical world, it was much more intense and pleasing to him.

Nor was Callaway alone in his discovery of these tunnels. Many accomplished projectors have explored new worlds via similar cosmic holes. Robert Monroe, for instance, spent many of his astral journeys in the "higher worlds." He describes his discovery of these cosmic tunnels in his *Journeys Out of the Body*. His initial discovery occurred while he was OBEing from his bed one night. Next to his bed he found a hole. "That's the only way to describe it," he writes. "To my sense, it seemed to be a hole in a wall which was about two feet thick and stretched endlessly in all directions." The brave explorer peered through the hole, but could not see anything but darkness, so he returned to his body.

During subsequent weeks, however, he cautiously investigated the hole and speculated as to where it might lead. Sometimes he would thrust his hands beyond the hole's edges and a friendly helper would grab them and help him through. But even after getting through, Monroe still faced total darkness.

Only during the next year did this "world beyond the hole"clear and become more definitive. This is probably because Monroe had begun allowing his mind to experience a new level of reality. The projector was able to dart through the hole and found himself near a barnlike structure surrounded by a gorgeous meadow. After exploring this new environment for a time, he reapproached the hole. Everything went black, and he found that he had re-entered his body.

Monroe had discovered a parallel universe; one that closely resembled our own, although much more beautiful. Eventually he discovered a misty, dreary world as well, a world other astral projectors have also encountered but found distasteful.

Whiteman, whose penetrating writings and theories first prompted me to accept the theory of interlocking universes, writes about what he calls "spatial openings," which closely resemble the holes that confronted Callaway and Monroe. Usually Whiteman sees these openings before he even leaves his body and is still in a preprojecting state. Then he projects directly through them. Here is his description of one such OBE:

> The separation [OBE] began with a "spatial opening" in which the surface of a whitewashed wall, two feet away, was studied, with a full clarity of perception and the visual impression of precise spatial position . . . The opening then changed to one in which heathlike country was seen in a wide panorama, with steep ground in front, and almost at once I was conscious for a few moments of being catapulted amid that scene.

A remarkable consistency exists among the reports of Monroe, Callaway, Forhan, and others about the way these higher worlds manifest. Many habitual projectors talk about three different worlds one might contact during the OBE. One is a world closely resembling our own. They believe that it is our world, while others have come to interpret it as a parallel world. The next is uniformly described as a dim, misty, almost hellish environment, which is definitely unpleasant. The third world is one of great beauty and suggests a garden of Eden. Sometimes spirits of the dead are seen there.

Luckily, these dimensions are not experienced solely by people proficient at leaving the body. Some individuals who have undergone spontaneous OBEs have contacted them as well, although quite by accident. Robert Crookall collected several accounts and presented them in his several casebooks.

A typical chance encounter with such a paradise world was reported at the turn of the century by J. W. Skilton. A railway engineer working in Jacksonville, Florida, at the time, Skilton later explained to investigators that he was loading crates one day when suddenly a radiant apparitional being appeared at his side. The being beckoned him to follow, and soon the startled engineer found himself floating over the countryside. A vast panorama of beauty spread beneath him. In the distance he saw a glittering world. "The beauties . . . were beyond any human being to describe," he later wrote. Skilton alighted there and found himself surrounded by music and more apparitions. He recognized some of them as dead and departed relatives. But before he could make contact with them, his radiant companion reappeared and whisked him back to his body.

Skilton's co-workers told the startled man that for the past several minutes he had not uttered a single word. He had merely carried on his tedious work with unbelievable ease. They laughed at his fantastic story, but Skilton later retold it to F. W. H. Myers, the pioneer psychical investigator and scholar who was then helping to organize the Society for Psychical Research in England. Myers was so impressed by the report and Skilton's obvious sincerity that he included it in his two-volume classic, *Human Personality and its Survival of Bodily Death.*

It would be fruitless to speculate on the range and number of OBE dimensions that may exist within the totality of the universe. For every one we know about, many more may exist totally beyond any earthly comprehension. Nonetheless, so many astral projectors have given basically similar descriptions of these dimensions that we are presented with a virtual cartography of the "higher worlds."

These might be worlds of real substance, too, even if they do seem beyond the reach of most of us. One is tempted to wonder whether two people simultaneously projecting to one of these worlds would report the same sights, sounds, and states of mind after returning to the body. A few accounts on record suggest that such would be the case. Forhan, Callaway, and Harary have projected to these dimensions along with wives or friends and noted similarities in their observations upon their return to the body. For example, the following experience has been reported by Keith Harary, and I see no reason to doubt his claims:

For some time I had been accustomed to having out-of-body experiences at times when I was otherwise asleep. Then about a year ago [1971] I shared a particularly interesting experience with my closest friend.

During waking hours before the experience I had been remembering an old woman friend who was separated from me by time and distance. I felt a strong personal desire to speak to this woman, to find out how she had been doing and to let her know that all was well with me.

After I fell asleep that night, I found myself floating out of my body which lay below me on the bed. I had this experience many times in the past and so was not surprised at its recurrence. I was, however, thankful for its occurrence at the time because this meant to me that I could travel while out of my body to find my old woman friend who was in Maine at the time while I was in New York.

Before I left the area to find the woman, one of my spiritual guides remarked to me that I should bring my close friend George with me on my out-of-body journey to Maine. I concentrated on George and soon was floating above him where he lay asleep on his bed. I awoke George's out-of-body self and he held out his hands to me and smiled. I grasped George's hands and pulled him up out of his body, which remained still on the bed below us. I informed George of my traveling plans and he readily decided to accompany me. None of this seemed the least bit unusual to either of us while we were in our out-of-body states.

George and I passed through some sort of an atmospheric barrier and entered another level of existence. From this level, the distance to Maine seemed much shortened, and we could walk there in a few hours. On the way to Maine, George and I walked through wooded areas, and up and down green, rolling hills. At one point when we stopped to rest on a hillside which was near our destination, George began to wander too close to a pool of pink, hot bubbling liquid. I warned George not to wander too close to the pool because it was very dangerous, even while in an OBE state.

We reached an area through which we could pass to return to our original Earth level and be in Maine near where we thought the woman we sought would be.

To their surprise, the two projectors found that their friend had also projected and met them out-of-body in this higher world. She was elderly, had reddish-blond hair, and high cheekbones. They all spoke together for some time, and then Blue accompanied George back to his body (via a passageway out of the higher world), and then returned to his New York home and re-entered his own;

I didn't see George again until later on the next day. (He was in his physical body, and so was I.) When he first saw me an odd expression passed over his face and he began to speak my name and to start a sentence which he forgot in the middle of speaking it. Not mentioning the night before, I asked him what was wrong. He said that when he awoke in the morning he had the strangest sensation of having forgotten something. He said he couldn't figure out what it was that he could have forgotten but that the sensation was overwhelming to him. I didn't offer him any clues. He also said that when he had first seen me a few moments ago a brief flash of "something" hit him and then he "lost what it was or what it meant." It wasn't until very much later in the evening when George remembered what had happened the night before.

He was sitting on his living room floor when a sudden strange look came across his face (he had been discussing dreams). His expression seemed at once to convey fear, awe, and bliss. He held his hands over his eyes and then pointed a finger at me and looking up with a shocked expression said "last night!" I looked at him trying to maintain composure and not yet show him the joy which I experienced at his apparent sudden recall of our mutual OBE experience. "Yes?" I asked him. He then proceeded to ask me if we had been out of our bodies together the previous night and if what seemed so real to him at the time actually was a real experience. I told him very little at first and asked him to tell me all of the details that he could remember. "A lady," he said; "there was this fantastic lady." "Was she an elderly lady?" I asked him. "Yes, but not with gray hair like most old ladies," he answered; "with reddish blond hair and with high cheekbones." I asked him about the experience we had while resting on the hill. He remembered that there had been a danger there and seemed to remember the pink, bubbling liquid from my description of it after he mentioned "something about a pool." From what we could piece together, both George and I shared the same out of body journey that evening.

The lesson we can learn from all this information is pretty obvious—a lesson that will become clear to you as you use the OBE for your own spiritual transformation. The universe and its various dimensions cannot be studied merely by the cold art of scientific measurements and statistics. It can be studied only by those who have experienced the various domains of the cosmos at first hand.

Even with all its limitations, science is a marvelous art. From its advances have come the great citadels of industry, technology, and worldly knowledge. But these noble citadels have become polluted by dungeons of horror. Nuclear arms, modern materialism, and the rejection of spiritual values serve to remind us of science's double-edged legacy. Voyaging inward and outward—through zen, meditation, yoga, and out-of-body travel—may not lead to any great scientific advancement on our part. But these practices may lead to a cultural revolution—a return to the primal spirituality with which humankind is endowed and which the materialism and hedonism of modern society has sought to smother. No wonder that people who have personally experienced out-of-body travel are overwhelmed by the religiosity of the experience. Their out-of-body journeys, although perhaps sparked by mere curiosity, soon become guided by a sense of moral duty and religious responsibility. Experiencing the higher worlds *is* a religious experience.

Learning the byways of time and space may turn the normal world of the five senses a bit topsy-turvy. But when one embarks on what is essentially a spiritual quest, that is a small price to pay.

REFERENCES

Crookall, Robert. *The Interpretation of Cosmic and Mystical Experiences.* London: James Clarke, 1969.

Fox, Oliver. *Astral Projection.* New Hyde Park, N.Y.: University Books, 1962 (reprint).

Johnson, Raynor. *Watcher on the Hills.* London: Hodder & Stoughton, 1959.

Monroe, Robert. *Journeys Out of the Body.* Garden City, N.Y.: Doubleday, 1970.

Myers, F. W. H. *Human Personality and its Survival of Bodily Death.* London: Longmans, 1903.

Palmer, John. Consciousness localized in space outside the body. *Osteopathic Physician,* 1974, *14,* 51-62.

————. The out-of-body experience: a psychological theory. *Parapsychology Review,* 1978, *5,* no. 9, 19-22.

Poynton, John. Parapsychology in South Africa. In *Parapsychology Today: A Geographical View.* New York: Parapsychology Foundation, 1973

Ring, Kenneth. *Life at Death.* New York: Coward, McCann, Georgegan, 1981.

Rogo, D. Scott. Experiments with Blue Harary. In *Mind Beyond the Body*, D. Scott Rogo, ed. New York: Penguin, 1978.

_____ . The out-of-body experience: some personal views and reflections. In *Mind Beyond the Body*.

_____ . Out-of-body dimensions. In *Other Worlds, Other Universes*, Brad Steiger and John White, eds. Garden City, N.Y.: Doubleday, 1975.

Sabom, Michael. *Recollections of Death*. New York: Harper & Row, 1982

Twemlow, Stuart. Epilogue: Personality profile. In *Journeys Out of the Body* by Robert Monroe. Garden City, N.Y.: Anchor/Doubleday, 1977.

Twemlow, Stuart, Gabbard, Glen, and Jones, Fowler. The out-of-body experience: II Phenomenology. Paper delivered at the 1980 meeting of the American Psychiatric Association.

Whiteman, J. H. M. *The Mystical Life*. London: Faber & Faber, 1961.

Bibliography

For more general information on the out-of-body experience, the following books may be consulted. There was a surge of parapsychological interest and research into the byways of the OBE in the early 1970s, so books written after 1974 will be more complete and useful.

Battersby, H. Prevost, *Man Outside Himself.* New Hyde Park, N.Y.: University Books, 1969 (reprint).

Black, David, *Ekstasy: out-of-the-body experiences.* New York: Bobbs-Merrill, 1975.

Blackmore, Susan, *Beyond the Body.* London: Heinemann, 1982.

Green, Celia, *Out-of-the-Body Experiences.* Oxford: Institute of Psychophysical Research, 1968.

Greenhouse, Herbert, *The Astral Journey.* Garden City, N.Y.: Doubleday, 1975.

Mitchell, Janet, *Out-of-Body Experiences—a handbook.* Jefferson, N.C.: McFarland, 1981.

Rogo, D. Scott, *Mind Beyond the Body.* New York: Penguin, 1978.

Shirley, Ralph, *The Mystery of the Human Double.* New Hyde Park, N.Y.: University Books, 1965 (reprint).

Smith, Susy, *The Enigma of Out-of-Body Travel.* New York: Garrett, 1965.

Index